STRATEGIES FOR CLASSROOM MANAGEMENT
K – 6

Making Magic Happen

Darlene Anderson Wilson

ScarecrowEducation
Lanham, Maryland • Toronto • Oxford
2004

Published in the United States of America
by ScarecrowEducation
An imprint of The Rowman & Littlefield Publishing Group, Inc.
4501 Forbes Boulevard, Suite 200, Lanham, Maryland 20706
www.scarecroweducation.com

PO Box 317
Oxford
OX2 9RU, UK

British Library Cataloguing in Publication Information Available

Library of Congress Cataloging-in-Publication Data

Wilson, Darlene Anderson, 1935–
  Strategies for classroom management, K–6 : making magic happen /
Darlene Anderson Wilson.
     p. cm.
  Includes bibliographical references.
  ISBN 1-57886-136-5 (pbk. : alk. paper)
 1. Classroom management—California—Los Angeles—Case studies.
 2. Elementary school teaching—California—Los Angeles—Case studies.
I. Title.
LB3013.W545 2004
371.102'4—dc22

                                                                2004000799

∞™ The paper used in this publication meets the minimum requirements of
American National Standard for Information Sciences—Permanence of Paper
for Printed Library Materials, ANSI/NISO Z39.48-1992.
Manufactured in the United States of America.

CONTENTS

FOREWORD

From what we hear everyone wants our educational system to be better. One hears about the need for more discipline in our schools and the desire for higher academic standards. There is also a demand for the return of values to the schoolroom.

Now we have a book that shows how one teacher achieved "miracles." *Strategies for Classroom Management K–6*, the result of more than thirty-eight years of teaching and teacher training, spells out how a classroom teacher can promote an atmosphere where the students not only succeed academically, but are eager to do their best while concentrating on the basic values of respect, responsibility, consideration, and sensitivity.

Darlene Wilson's story of her students' successes in the classroom during the last half of the twentieth century is stimulating reading as well as a marvelous teaching tool.

This book represents an inspiring and informative quixotic journey— a path where a teacher maintained excellence in academic achievement and student behavior while tilting at the windmills of societal change in the last half of the Twentieth Century.

Parents, teachers, teacher trainers, students, and even the public will want to read this exciting book.

Dr. Joseph Schieffer

ACKNOWLEDGMENTS

Many thanks go to my husband, Chuck, without whom this book would never have been written. It was he who kept after me to take the classroom happenings and students' successes and put them on paper.

I am very grateful to my son, Scott, the first reader of my manuscript. He encouraged me and gave me technical support.

Former coworkers Don Sanuskar and Joyce Stephenson kept me focused as they conferred with me on chapters about the bilingual and mentally gifted students. Graduate professors Dr. Michael Berliner, Dr. Justine Su, and Dr. Dudley Blake were instrumental in encouraging me and helping me. Dr. Joseph Schieffer graciously wrote a foreword, and I thank him for his interest.

To Stephanie Lawrence I owe a great debt as she helped me make sure that I had a clean manuscript. Mindy Lees, Dale Ellis, Leslie Timber, Naicong Li, Eugene Jacobowitz, and Laurie and John Viola were instrumental in giving me technical support. Zinet Aboubaker was always helpful in the day-to-day need for copies, paper, etc. Enthusiasm and ongoing support from Marlyn Taber, Israel Minick, and Arlene Schaupp kept me going.

I could always count on Tom Koerner, my editor, to immediately give me valuable feedback. What a fantastic help. I so appreciate his support throughout the process.

Many thanks to all of you for your involvement in this story. As was my teaching, this book has been a community endeavor.

INTRODUCTION

This book tells how one can have an exciting, challenging career in the elementary classroom. It is a teaching tool. I spent my professional life as a teacher and acting principal in elementary schools in the Los Angeles Unified School District.

During the decades that ranged from the fifties through the nineties, I found that the students in my classes—from kindergarten through sixth grade—were having phenomenal success in their academic progress, as well as in the affective domain. In the seventies, I saw this unusual level of achievement in a class for mentally gifted students, and in the eighties I observed it in my bilingual class.

My classes were so well behaved that they were a pleasure to greet every morning. What appeared to be an exceptional level of excellence in my classroom year after year did not always seem to be the norm in the classrooms around me.

Our society went through many changes while I was teaching. These changes made a difference in how students were prepared to study in school, and how much their families were able to help them.

The schools in Los Angeles started to become multicultural during the seventies. Different ethnicities and languages brought new needs to the classroom that were not there in the fifties. Working parents appeared to be the norm in the eighties, and parents had less time to spend with their children. Today there is much concern over crime in society, and many children are not as carefree as they once were.

Curiosity led me to analyze why my students were excelling, why they were so happy and secure much of the time while they were in my class, and why after thirty-eight years I was not burned out. As society went through changes, I had to make adjustments to address the children's needs, but I never stopped wanting each boy and girl to achieve his or her potential.

The first part of this book deals with where American schools are now in their quest for academic success in the classroom. Part 1 questions whether society really can agree on success, and it shows how one can arrange the activities and discipline in one's classroom in order to gain a high level of academic achievement as well as good behavior and a sense of comradeship among the students in the class.

The second part of the book shows how important the concept of the classroom as a community has become since the eighties. Students do not learn in a vacuum. A climate for learning must be established that fosters a sense of security and enthusiasm for studying and exploring. There are four chapters that explain how to promote a special sense of community.

This section also analyzes the changes in society that were reflected in the classroom during the decades I taught. The second half of the twentieth century saw much upheaval that changed the structure and direction of the schools. It was a period that began with Sputnik and progressed to "tomato seeds from space."

Some of the changes in society are further described in part 3, which starts with a view of the history of public education in America and follows with examples of special programs for the mentally gifted and the bilingual. Since the mass media are so influential, I have included the classroom teacher's image in television series to show how the changes that influenced the schools have been reflected in the media.

As a training teacher for the Department of Education at California State University, Northridge, for thirty years, I believe that many of the successes the young people in my classes have achieved can be duplicated. The last part of this book can be used as a manual for new teachers or student teachers that want the best for the students in their elementary school classes. It has specific ideas to help teachers, parents, and others interested in the well-being of young children.

PART I

Americans need to clarify whether they really want academic success for their young people. If they do, these chapters show ways that teachers and parents can assure high achievement for their students and children.

1

DO AMERICANS REALLY WANT ACADEMIC SUCCESS?

This is a book that shows how young students can attain phenomenal success. Here you will find explanations of how pupils can rise above current expectations. I kept wondering why the students in my classes were praised so highly by everyone, why these young people were succeeding far above the norm.

I am thrilled to be able to say that I have seen boys and girls achieve incredible academic success. These children attended the public schools in Los Angeles, California. This is the story of more than a thousand kindergartners and first through sixth graders whose progress I observed during the fifties, sixties, seventies, eighties, and nineties. Within these five decades many social changes took place. As the students in my classroom reflected these changes, new techniques to promote success had to be developed.

What teachers don't want their classroom experience to be a journey of bliss and wonder? What a thrill to have pupils and their parents tell you that you have made a difference in a student's life. Teaching is a job that can be all-encompassing, exciting, and satisfying. What is teaching? Teaching is encouraging others to reach their potential. Every day, year after year, meeting the children as they come into the classroom can be an adventure. The experience can always be a rewarding challenge that never becomes tiresome.

During those thirty-eight years of watching individual students reach and stretch to accomplish wonders, I was aware that the success these boys and girls achieved was not universal. I wondered why the pupils in my room scored higher than expected on tests and why their classroom behavior was so good. I began to question if the society in which I lived and worked wanted success, because the achievement that I saw meant that the students had to persevere, put time into the task, and think that it was all a worthwhile endeavor.

Much has recently been written and discussed about the lack of academic prowess in American test results. Does this mean everyone wants American students to achieve their potential? Does it mean we are willing to think of success as related to hard work and perseverance? I had always assumed that everyone wanted young people to perform at their top academic level. Unfortunately, experience in the American school system taught me otherwise. It is almost as though excellence is sometimes suspect.

On March 31, 1991, a public broadcasting station's television documentary "Quest for Education" showed that Japanese students emphasize passing high school exams and group conformity, spend many hours studying and doing homework, and welcome parental drive to help get into a good university. The following days, April 1, 1991, and April 2, 1991, the same public broadcasting channel presented a special two-part program titled "America's Schools: Who Gives a Damn?" The American students interviewed put emphasis on their extracurricular activities, the importance of friendships, and having fun. The message seemed to be that performing well academically in school was not the prime consideration.

Americans do not have agreed-upon values. Some developed countries do have common values. This becomes very evident when reviewing the literature in the comparative education field. Since a country's economic success is seen as closely correlating to its educational system's success, many texts and research papers are now being written on comparative education. In the nineties, this new field appeared in university class offerings.

A quick overview of comparative education studies shows that most developed nations have a common objective of educational success. It is a national goal. Such aims are easier to achieve in countries that have a common set of values. Excellence in education became such a popular topic of concern in the nineties that a local radio station, in conjunction with a local newspaper, held a grassroots forum at a neighborhood public library in Los Angeles. There was a panel composed of a Los Angeles School Board member and some local politicians. After the panel members introduced themselves and spoke briefly about the state of education, the public was invited to ask questions. They asked if the panel members were not disturbed by our country's lack of agreed-upon standards for education, especially since there seems to be such an economic connection between education and a country's financial well-being. It seemed that they, too, were concerned.

A local radio station in Los Angeles, KNX, even has spot announcements, called "Classroom Focus," that tell the public about students and schools. So, although it is difficult to turn on the radio, listen to the news, or peruse the magazine rack without hearing or seeing the high level of media coverage about education, its merits and pitfalls, we still do not seem to have a consensus on the following question: Do we, as Americans, want our students to achieve academic success? If the answer is yes, what are we willing to do to achieve it?

A good teacher always wants the pupils in his or her class to achieve their potential in many areas, including academic success. Many of the one thousand plus boys and girls who were in my classes showed fantastic growth in their academic prowess. This book is the story of their success and how that success can be achieved in today's classrooms.

IS IT MAGIC, MIRACLES, OR MOTIVATION?

The academic success of students is very exciting to watch. But who are the achievers? How do they get to be the most accomplished? What motivates them to a high level of attainment? Are only English speakers from two-parent families achievers?

In the fifties, parents motivated their children to do well in school. That was a lovely, ideal situation. Teaching was a lot less tiring then, but not necessarily more satisfying. By the nineties some teachers discovered that quite often they had a much greater desire for the students to be successful than did the children's families. This was a startling revelation. One hopes that parents and principals would all want students to excel academically, to be very successful.

This was not always the case. An example is the single parent who prefers to have his or her daughter help take care of the preschool cousins so that the cousins' mother can work. Since the parent is self-employed and working at home, the daughter stays at home to handle the housework and other chores. This kind of parent seems pleased to have his or her daughter placed in a special education program for students several grades below the norm. Someone has to do all the housework, so the daughter's homework, whether for her regular class or her special education class, just never gets finished.

If the teacher wants more for this student than her father or mother wants for her, the parent–teacher relationship becomes tense. Why this father or mother never approves of his or her daughter's slow, steady progress toward a higher level of academic achievement is puzzling. Is it a threat to families when a child performs well academically? Do they prefer a low level of achievement? Is that why there was no satisfaction exhibited when academic success was achieved?

I also wonder why some principals seem to lack interest in hearing about students' exceptional academic growth and excellence. Rocketing test scores almost seem to embarrass some of them. One possible answer is that administrators, as well as the general public, have become so accustomed to a lowering of expectations, of children receiving A grades and comments of "excellent" on work that is below standard, that they can fail to perceive that a real difference has occurred.

It seems that society became accustomed to a lowering of expectations during the social revolt of the sixties. The revolt that was brought about by the rigidity of the fifties was the beginning of many changes. Remembering the sixties brings to mind hippies, new music, a sense of "doing your own thing," body painting, *Laugh-In*, and long hair. This period of social change certainly emphasized the American myth of individualism. It was an exciting, heady time. It seemed to be a time of promise, a time of better things to come, such as peace and brotherhood. Sisterhood was to come later. These changes had a sense of excitement. Many remember seeing the musical *Hair* and singing the lyrics as they walked along the boulevard to their car. There was a great urge to grab the strangers around them, give them a hug, and continue skipping down the street. It was a time of great energy. Doing your own thing, sleeping in a loft or a pad with dozens of friends while experimenting with drugs did not lead to enthusiasm about schoolwork. Success in the classroom seemed to become irrelevant.

While the sixties released many from the feeling of social restraints and values connected to the post–World War II period, the seventies and the Vietnam War brought about an ongoing rage toward authority figures. Institutions and those connected to them were seen as thwarting the general populace's freedom. Schools and law enforcement agencies were obvious targets for this new antiauthoritarianism. Additionally, the Vietnam War caused many students to plead their case to professors:

If they did not get a passing grade, they would have to go to "Nam." Grade inflation had begun. Many professors cried out in alarm, but the social pressure was great and real.

Many were surrounded by these changes. Some attended peace marches, and others worried about the idea of a son or a daughter having to go to war. But, even in chaotic times, one can take a quixotic path and keep on emphasizing high standards, both academic and social, in the classroom. It can indeed be a quixotic path when it seems as though very few people are still interested in success based on responsibility and hard work.

In a way, I suspect it is exciting to try for the impossible. It certainly keeps one at a heightened level of purpose. Expecting and demanding from students a level of hard work, acceptable achievement, and determination in order to get passing grades may not always seem to be the norm in today's schools. Today, newspapers, magazines, and television specials continue to cry out about our national standards being too low in comparison to those of other developed nations. National, state, and city standards of achievement are discussed. Committees draw up guidelines that are then debated but not resolved. Meanwhile, I suspect that, as a nation, we are not sure that we consider academic excellence to be a national goal. Why else would many principals and families be nonplussed about individual and group achievement?

As family structure changed during the last half of the twentieth century, teachers found themselves filling the void. Many did not want to see students slip through the cracks of indifference. It is important to ask of individual students that which they are capable of achieving. The good teacher becomes the one who wants them to achieve. The question is, how can teachers get students to achieve what they are capable of if no one else is interested, including the students themselves?

Motivation seems to be the answer. A teacher has to devise some way to make students want to have academic success, make it worth their while. Through close observation, it becomes obvious that "free" classroom time spent with classmates on exciting projects serves as a good motivation. Students can earn this free time by studying well enough the first time an assignment is given. Extra drill is then not necessary for those students. They then have free time to explore challenging logic puzzles, read literature, and work on advanced and involved art projects.

Those who are successful get the reward of more interesting work. It also allows the teacher to develop a program where those who need to study more have that time.

It works! Here is a very successful technique using the above philosophy. Those who achieve a score of 90 percent or above on the test can be in the Math Club until the next test is given in three or four weeks' time. Math Club students do not have to review the new math lesson with the teacher as the others do. After an introductory lesson of twenty to thirty minutes, they are dismissed to computer challenges, origami, free reading, board games, free art, or paper airplane building. After the math instruction for the day is over, those who make paper airplanes can show off how well their models fly. Sometimes the competition might be to get the plane to sail across the room into a walk-through closet or to perform aerobatic tricks before landing. The paper airplane designs can be an outgrowth of a science lesson on aerodynamics. This extra experimentation time allows the students to put into practice the principles they have studied.

Imagine a student who has never done well in math before he or she comes to the United States from El Salvador. The student's family wants the son or daughter to do well, but the child does not respond to the parents' desires. Unfortunately the student has so-so or failing grades on his or her math tests. One can begin to see a frustrated look on this student's face when he or she gets the corrected math test back. Then it happens. The child gets a 100 percent score on a math test. A good class will cheer as they do for everyone who is new to the Math Club. How can this happen? Later that day, when you can talk privately, ask how the student has done so much better this time. The teacher can expect to be glared at, while the student puts hands on hips, stamps a foot on the floor, and states in a most emphatic tone of voice, "I studied for three hours."

That is the payoff! The motivation works. This student has discovered that he or she has the ability. One just has to apply oneself. Later, similar successes can be had without quite as much study time. This student has learned that hard work brings success. That leads to an important question. Do we, as Americans, have a national reference or ancestral heritage for applying ourselves as individuals to a task? Is that an American trait? Or is it a trait only found in other cultures, such as the Japanese? If much of our national heritage and our social institutions, including the family, have not primed us to be highly motivated in a search for success in academics, it would seem that the teacher on the quixotic path needs to find "magic" motivation and then watch the miracles develop.

3

TEACHING IS AN
ART—NOT A SCIENCE

Teachers become aware of the truthfulness of the above statement as they try to explain to a group of parents why some children do better than others. If teaching was a science every teacher could predict each child's grade and performance, and there would be no variation. Teachers would select the data, store it in their brains, and retrieve it. It just doesn't work that way.

Smart teachers learn to use all the tricks that the students themselves will teach them. Try many different techniques for each subject, varying the structure as each new need arises. It certainly is a job to stay on one's toes. It is the art or creative part of the job that offers a teacher stimulation and challenge. Sometimes it seems that a daily reorganization of plans and structure is necessary to achieve the most from the situation. This can be exciting and rewarding. It is up to us, as teachers and parents, to do this for students. Not that it is easy, but the rewards of seeing students respond and succeed are definitely worth it.

One often sees how simple it would be for the teacher to follow through, but unfortunately it just isn't done. Imagine a teacher specifically telling a group of students to *walk* to the playground equipment on the yard. Then the teacher turns her back on the students and goes into her classroom. There is no reason for them to walk as no one cares enough to watch them. Those children, as they run to the equipment, will eye other adults on the yard suspiciously, as if to ask: Are we suppose to get away with this? An observer would want to assure them that it should be an ordered universe and say, "I think she wanted you to walk." Personally, I would advise them to run as fast as they want, for if the yard is empty, it's helpful for them to understand when it is a good time to run.

THE ART OF HELPING EVERY CHILD
TO EMPOWERMENT

All teachers need to remember how important it can be to a child to feel that they are properly acknowledged. Imagine a child named Gloria. When Gloria's classmates raise their hands to answer questions or volunteer to take on tasks, Gloria's hand will be up, but her facial expression will be strained and unhappy. A good teacher will wonder why Gloria, who might be one of thirty-five bright fifth graders, is so tense. Let's assume that Gloria is an attractive, taller-than-average student, of Italian and Mexican heritage.

Gloria's class is probably one of those classes where the students have been together since kindergarten. A small group of these students might have been identified as gifted students. Bright students in California are identified and have access to what is termed the Gifted and Talented program (GATE). It is a special program designed for the mentally gifted, high-achieving, and talented child. It seems that Gloria feels she was not chosen to answer questions or take on tasks as often as the students in the GATE cluster. Gloria has not been identified as a GATE student, but she is very bright and extremely capable. A good teacher's sense of fairness will mean that Gloria will be called upon as often as anyone else. Then will such a child bloom into a student whose competence is noted and appreciated.

Let's assume that Gloria has exceptional literary ability. When she saw that her writing talent was being acknowledged equally with those of the group that she had always felt was getting all the attention and accolades, she became less tense in appearance and became a source of enjoyment and leadership to herself and those around her. I would expect that the above teacher would be able to treasure the written note of appreciation given to her at the end of Gloria's fifth-grade year. It is a smart move to have these notes of appreciation also sent to the principal or administrator.

Sometimes, though, giving a bright student extra responsibility is not the right approach for that child. Again, teaching is an art, not a science. It is hard to always know exactly the right mix of involvement for each child. College classes leading to a degree in education and a teaching credential do not always let one know how sensitive a child can be when given the responsibility to be the leader of her kindergarten class in a winter pageant.

This time, let's imagine a precocious five-year-old at a school in the Mulholland Hills area. When the school's principal and staff are told that Gayle can read anything put in front of her, they show disbelief until she goes to the office and reads some of the principal's manuals out loud. She is a student who has no peer at her intellectual level in that particular class. The teacher tries to make the day's lesson stimulating to her. When the class is shown a picture for their language development, the teacher would also engage Gayle in a short dialogue. One can imagine this teacher and student discussing planetary movements in the galaxy in a few quick sentences while the other children are preparing themselves to answer a simpler question.

As the winter program's date nears, Gayle seems to be the perfect student to lead her class onto the stage as they circle a tree before they sing "Jingle Bells." She could quickly understand the importance of the cue to get on stage, and her teacher knew she would not forget. What that teacher's inexperience in the art of teaching led to was tears in Gayle's eyes. The day of the performance the school auditorium was packed, and Gayle's classmates, waiting in the wings of the stage, were so excited that she feared they would not watch her and would not do it correctly. She was anxious. It turned out just right, but the strain of making sure it was just right was too much for that particular child. Good teachers must be aware that a child who is bright and can remember everything can still be overburdened by being made responsible for others his or her age.

Sometimes what happens when a teacher plans to help a student in the classroom comes as a complete surprise. An unplanned event can turn into a successful conclusion. Imagine a student whose father has recently died. This student needs to have a more relaxed sense of herself among her classmates. She is new to the class when her father dies. The teacher might even know the family as he or she has taught the older brother and sister. It would not be unusual for the teacher to be at the funeral. The teacher might even find that it was her hand that the grieving child held onto outside the church as people milled around at the memorial service.

A teacher would feel compassion for the child's predicament and, perhaps without being aware of it, would show a certain amount of solicitousness to her in class. After a few months it became obvious that she was not doing well in classwork nor was she getting along well with her classmates. Let's assume that this was a class that was especially well behaved and self-motivated, and the teacher rarely had to remind them to get on task. One day, without consciously being aware of what the outcome might be, the teacher suddenly spoke sharply and loudly to tell the still-grieving child to get to work. All eyes that had been attentive to work in the room were suddenly focused on the withdrawn child. One could sense that the class, too, had felt that this girl needed special treatment due to her father's death. Somehow, by treating her just like everyone else, the tension that had built up around this child was released. She relaxed, and her classmates could now treat her as just one of the group. This kind of experience reinforces the idea of teaching as an art.

TIMING IS AN ART

While we may want the same level of success for each child, the children themselves can be on different, individual time schedules, and they do listen to their own drummers. The art of teaching includes helping children advance from a position where they seem to be stuck or at a plateau in their development. With a young person, it seems an individual approach is necessary. In a multigraded class you might find a student who is bright and has lots of interests and motivation. Socially, he isn't sure about playing softball with the rest of the class, even though he is not the youngest. The other children are eager to play, as regardless of age, most of them were in some sort of after-school Little League–type program. It becomes obvious by his body language and his reluctance that he is not yet secure in this area. It is your job to find a way to show him that he has the ability to master the task. It is more of a concern on his part of not feeling comfortable with the situation than a matter of native ability.

You can develop a plan to get him to be a participant at a safe level. This will let him feel less of an isolate and more a part of the whole group while still maintaining the sense of security he needs. The first step is to have him be in charge of record keeping. You can have him sit on the bench next to you, where you are calling strikes and balls. He can keep the game score for you. Classmates who are playing will look over his shoulder to check the score. His importance to the game has started.

Next, you can talk him into helping you at first base. This will be about a week later. It is a real need, and that makes a difference, as he is smart enough to perceive the importance of the task. It needs to be a legitimate concern. You can't always see whose foot gets on the base first, the runner or the baseman. By being at the spot, he can see if the runner is safe or out. This gives him involvement on the playing field. He is still physically close to you, and he is on the outside of the baseline.

This can be a very successful move. As the class can only play if they are respectful of each other's roles, which includes fair play, others start to depend on him to help make first-base decisions. You may even notice by his swagger and smile that he is beginning to feel more comfortable in what had been a foreign arena. The next step may be initiated by him. He might want to try watching third base for a while. After that week, you can quietly, privately, say to him that you think it is time for him to play and let the others take turns at his job. It works. It works so well that years later, you can expect to see him in a role of social leadership that has become a natural for him.

Perhaps it is this very concept of teaching as an art that makes it so difficult for university departments of education to devise programs that actually teach education majors how to teach. There are methods that help. Some of these techniques are listed in the last part of this book. Most of all, the teacher has to pay a great deal of attention to the particular group he or she is teaching each year. Probably, one could teach first grade for twenty years and hardly ever have a similar type of class. It is this refined adjustment to a particular group's needs that lends itself to success, creativity, and challenge.

HEY EVERYBODY OUT THERE! JOHNNY CAN READ, AND SO CAN JUAN AND JOSE!

Picture a happy, relaxed, eager class every morning, a class where many students better their standardized test scores in the year they are with you. What a tremendous sense of satisfaction it is to see children realize their individual potential. You *can* make it happen.

The first week of the school year, it is good to administer a standardized reading test to your fifth- or sixth-grade class. You will want a test that will give a reading comprehension score based on a vocabulary test. After you have eagerly scored the tests at home, you can individually counsel each boy and girl as to his or her score. It is best to always interpret scores as one test only, a useful tool for you and the student. The score does not reflect his or her value as a person; it just shows how he or she performed on a particular test, and there will be many more chances for the students to test themselves. You need to also advise them that it is a good idea not to brag or compare scores with anyone else, but it is fine to tell their parents.

The students need to understand that you aren't going to announce any particular score out loud with a name attached to it. Privacy and security are paramount in gaining children's trust. Why should they give their best if they don't find themselves in a safe situation? You can give the range of scores to the class and mention how many of them are reading above grade level. A sense of classroom pride can be so easily instilled if you use every occasion possible to remind them of how well they are doing as a group.

The students should understand that they will take the same test at the end of the school year. You will not teach any of the specific words on the test, as that will compromise your objective. Your intention is to give them difficult, thoughtful reading that encompasses comprehension daily as the year progresses. Some days the work can be in history, other days, in science or health. The result of reading to find answers, a process that ranks high on Bloom's Taxonomy (a rating of thinking skills, going from mere classification at the lowest to a top of synthesis), can be an exciting rise in the classroom's overall ability.

Individual children can simply amaze you and delight themselves and their families with fantastic success. I have seen that happen. I was able to tell a student that his reading ability had shown an increase equivalent to six years. He went from reading at the third-grade level to the ninth-grade level in the 180 days of school that I had to work with the class each year. Another student showed a gain of *nine* years. He rose from a score at the second-grade level in September to a score of eleventh grade in June. I was shocked and delighted. I know it was a valid test as he sat right next to my desk, a place where a child who needs extra attention from the teacher often sits. It is easier, quicker, and less intrusive to catch a student's eye when he is close by in order to get him back on task. This student's progress, I suspect, was a combination of my interest in his doing better, his father's interest, and his having the opportunity to read very carefully, with comprehension, in order to get a good grade on a test. These two boys from Mexico, who had learned Spanish as a first language, showed a success in reading English that society does not lead us to believe is generally possible. But it happened, and it happened often enough to be a pattern.

Students should not be reading randomly; good literature should be read, dramatized, and discussed. The excitement of learning is developed in this program at the same time that information is discovered and understood. Goals have to be clearly defined, making them easier to achieve. Report card grades in the academic areas of history, science, and health can be based mainly on how well students can assimilate the material read and discussed in class. They then have the opportunity to study the test questions beforehand in order to clarify their thinking and to determine how they will phrase their written answers. There can be a few multiple-answer questions, for example, to list the relevant parts of a component or match up the correct word with its meaning or interpretation. Correct answers on those types of questions should not be enough to get a passing grade of C. More in-depth-type answers, subjective answers written in response to difficult questions, should be needed in order to get a passing or higher grade. Some students won't have to study as much as others. It is as individual as the children themselves.

Some students will find that their numerical grade average is below what they would choose to have appear on their report card. One way to achieve an A or B, if that is their choice, is to study hard enough to get consistently good grades on tests. A number system is not as value oriented in some ways as a letter grade. Therefore, it is best to only list percentages on tests. Also, a 79 percent is almost 80 percent. That looks much more satisfactory than just a C. During the first week of school and on the night the parents come to meet the teacher, Back-to-School Night, it is good to list this simple formula on the board:

A is 100%–90%
B is 89%–80%
C is 79%–70%
D is 69%–60%
F is 59%–00%

Once the students realize that they, not the teacher, are in charge of the grade they get, they become excited about tests. They are challenged. And, best of all, they develop a sense of empowerment that is heady to watch. Think of the satisfaction of hearing young people on the playground discussing how they studied and what they think is the best answer to a question.

During each reporting period for the year, you can make available a list of extra-credit work and its point value. This work is above and beyond the necessary work. If done well, the student will receive a certain number of points that will be added to his or her total average for a subject. In science, a student might design a good-looking three-dimensional space station and write a thrilling science fiction story using the relevant science material the class has been studying. In this way, the student who is just waiting to be stimulated to show off his or her initiative can do extra work. Those who participate will seem to derive a great deal of pleasure from the experience. Meanwhile, the non-motivated student is not subject to embarrassment or work that may be beyond his or her capability at that time. It is a *win–win* situation that parents seem to greatly appreciate. You get the added pleasure of seeing how much pride the student's family got out of watching his work on his space projects. He did the work, and they got the enjoyment.

Always evaluate progress during the year. It is good to reflect to see if the students were challenged enough, overworked, or challenged too little. One objective criterion that you can depend on is the attendance records. Is the attendance in your class high compared to other classes? If yes, you can assume that the environment you have arranged for the students is working well for them. It is also wise to ask students how they judged the workload and level of work, and to listen to the parents' feedback. Every class is different. Each child is an individual. Remember to give each of them the opportunity for the fullest development.

As a parent, doesn't this sound like the dream you want for your child? It can happen. I know. For almost four decades I saw this happen year after year in my classroom. By now, you might be wondering what type of school, teacher, or students will be able to use the above suggestions. Do they have to be special students? No, the experience above was not based on out-of-the-ordinary students. They were a mixed group of about thirty-six fifth- or sixth-grade boys and girls with reading scores ranging from second-grade comprehension to twelfth-grade comprehension. All of this disparity was in the same room. Some children had family support at home. Some not only lacked support but also were abused. A handful of students had to ride on a bus an hour or more due to overcrowding at their local school. Family problems and financial problems were not limited to those students who came on a bus. Some of the local students' parents had suffered from Southern California's recession. Struggling single parents, male or female, were struggling to do their best in both parenting and working roles.

These classes, from the seventies through the nineties, were multicultural classes with about six or more different languages represented. *Yet*, year after year, these were the classrooms described in the above success paragraphs. As one student asked years after he'd been in my class, does this year's Room 5 still have that magic?

5

DISCIPLINE IS NOT A FOUR-LETTER WORD—IT IS A SENSE OF SECURITY AND ORDER

As a teacher you *can* have a class that is the best-behaved in the school, a class that has a sense of *community*. You *can* have students who perform better academically than they did the previous year. As a parent, you *can* want and get the best for your child. It is possible. Having aides point out how well-behaved my students were on the yard as well as in the classroom or auditorium almost became embarrassing. Coworkers would shrug and say, "Oh, your class is always quiet." Principals would grin and say, "Darlene will take care of the problem, just wait and see."

I, for my part, expected that the rowdiest child on the yard the previous year would show up in my class as the new school year began in September, and the challenge was always there. I would question myself: Can I help this young person? Is this an unreasonable expectation to ask of myself? Somehow, it always worked out. The troubled student became less disruptive.

Here is an example. After one year's most troubled child left with his family for another school in a different city before the term was out, I received many letters from him. This astonished me as much as his fellow classmates and all the administrators who had previously had to deal with his unruly and violent behavior. The important point here is that children like fairness, justice, a sense of security, reasonableness, and

consistent follow-through on the adult's part. Otherwise there is no reason for them to do as we ask.

Students respond to a sense of order in their world. This was easy to
see when I was acting principal as well as fifth-grade teacher. If the
principal was not on campus and an administrative decision was needed,
I was asked to do both activities at the same time, teach and adminis-
trate. I vividly remember an incident that happened more than once. A
few minutes before the morning bell rang, alerting students to line up
and go into their classrooms, I was called by the office to take care of another classroom as that teacher's substitute for the day had not shown
up. That meant there would be about seventy students, my class and the
other teacher's class, who needed to get into separate classrooms and be
supervised. The door to my classroom was already open, and I had a key
to the other classroom. Passing my class on the way to the unsupervised
class, I told my boys and girls that I had to help out. I gave my class permission to go ahead and go into our room. Then, I took the other students to their room down at the other end of the hallway and got them
settled until the substitute arrived about twenty minutes later.

Breathlessly, I ran back to my classroom, worrying about the loss of
time. We would be behind schedule. *Astonishment and delight!* The students had gone into the room. The classroom president had led the flag
salute, the paper monitors had passed out paper, and most children had
started working on the next assignment in math without a word of direction from me. The teacher and aide watching from the room across
the hall were just as surprised as I was to see that boys and girls do rise
to the situation if they have an ordered, reasonable routine. It was as important to them as it was to me to get on with the business of the day. I
complimented them on their terrific ability to get right to work. A sense
of well-being, satisfaction, and pride showed in their smiles and relaxed
work attitudes.

Seeing those students being responsible and showing initiative left
me with a sense of wonder. Then I realized that I had instituted certain
strategies for classroom management that led to young people taking
charge and being responsible. The strategies were developed over many
years. The boys and girls, themselves, and fellow teachers helped me see
the need for the techniques that are explained in detail in the last part
of this book.

6

WHY CAN'T WE AGREE ON SUCCESS?

The presidents of the United States and the nation's governors all seem to have great difficulty in agreeing about setting higher goals for our nation's schools. This ongoing problem of setting standards occurs because, as a nation, we do not have an agreed-upon value system. The governors tried to address the problems of history standards developed by the UCLA National Center for History in the Schools. Those standards had been attacked for slighting George Washington and traditional views of American progress.

The International Reading Association and the National Council of Teachers of English did not fare any better. There were attacks from many sides on the English standards drawn up by those groups. The standards were charged with being unreadable. I understand why there are no standards in English. For years, teachers have been told at seminars and in-service classes that the student is to just start writing. Spelling and correct punctuation, we were told, are not as important as the student getting his or her thoughts down on paper. This began to happen in the sixties and seventies, and some parents were amazed by teachers who wanted to correct creative writing during that period of time.

Parents would later tell teachers how upset they were when they saw that their child's writing had previously been graded as satisfactory when it was filled with errors. Teachers, following the school district's advice, would put comments on a paper as to the interest or thoughtfulness of the subject, but they ignored the errors. It was hard for parents to encourage their children to write correctly and well when the school system was not supporting them. Sometimes a teacher has to figure out what is the right path. You can develop students' writing skills and interest in writing, even if you point out that spelling and grammar are important. Parents are delighted and thankful when they see a teacher who can encourage writing and also emphasize correct spelling and grammar. Their astonishment and thankfulness are good reinforcements for the teacher who treads the lonely path of what is best for the child. Students should have the opportunity to write to express ideas. Boys and girls also need to have the assurance that their writing is correct. Students who have been taught with an emphasis on correct spelling and grammar tend to have exceptional success in their English classes in middle school.

The problem is how to address a school board's policy and have your former students write well enough that when they apply for a job with the Los Angeles Police Department, they are complimented on their superior writing skills. It is sometimes hard to balance the district's directives and what you think is truly correct and ethical into an English educational philosophy. That answer can be found by setting out exactly what is expected for a good grade when the students are given a writing assignment.

Give a percentage grade to the grammar and spelling part of the writing. Then, to balance the district's emphasis on encouraging students to write, write a complimentary comment on their paper. If a paper is poorly done and cannot pass the standards for fifth grade, the student can be given time to check the errors and rewrite it for a passing grade. While those children participate in rewriting, the other boys and girls have a less rigorous, less boring task. This makes it worth their while to do a good job. For some, it is a great motivation.

After you explain a creative or expository writing assignment, the students can be told how many points will be subtracted for each misspelled word and each incorrect comma or period. Make sure that points are taken off only on areas of English that have previously been taught and reviewed. Everyone in the classroom should keep their dictionaries on top of their desks. Elementary students have small desks, and they are crammed with texts, papers, and miscellaneous goodies. By insisting that the large dictionary stay on top of the desk at all times, you will know that it is always accessible.

Learning the fine points of grammar is not always interesting to children. Every year, I would see that run-on sentences, two or more independent clauses in one sentence, were still mystifying the students. It took a lot of review and a little "ham" to get them to pay attention to the importance of such minutiae. To really get their attention, I would run around the classroom while reciting a sentence that went on and on with many clauses without stopping for a breath. This caught their interest.

The grading system of taking off points for misspelled words and grammar problems works. After the students finish writing their assignment, they have the opportunity to proofread a classmate's paper and to ask the teacher for help. At this point, you can tell them which line has an error in it and see if they can find the problem. When the boys and girls are helping each other with spelling, the dictionaries are out and lots of discussion can go on about correct spellings.

It is exciting to watch students who are interested in arguing about perfect spelling. The game "Ghost," which I taught and used anytime the class had a few extra minutes before dismissal to recess or lunch, is a great developer of interest in spelling. Then the dictionary would again be a great source of information. Ghost is a game played by about three to six people. The first person thinks of a word and says the first letter of that word out loud. The next person thinks of a word starting with that letter and says the first two letters out load. This continues until any word is spelled correctly. The round is finished when a word, longer than three letters, is spelled correctly. The person who finished spelling the word loses that round. He or she is a third of a ghost. Another person then starts a new word. If a player thinks that there is no such word that is spelled with the letters *owt*, for example, then he or she calls, "Challenge." The person challenged has to spell the word he or she was thinking of. If needed, the dictionary is used to verify the existence of the word. If there is no such word, the challenged player loses the round and becomes a third of a ghost. Each time a player loses a challenge or ends a word (more than three letters long), he or she increases from a third of a ghost to two-thirds of a ghost to a ghost who is out of the game. The trick then is for the person out of the game to try and get the other players to talk to him or her. If they do, they are out of the game and ghosts also. The winner is the player who can continue to add additional letters without ending a word. For instance, instead of ending with the word *encourage*, one could turn the letters into *encouraging*. This stimulates vocabulary as well as spelling.

In each of these cases, taking points off for misspellings or playing a game, the object is to make correct spelling relevant. It has meaning or a payoff. Getting a good grade and seeing one's paper on the bulletin board or winning a game is the satisfying reward.

So even though there is a lack of unity among those who are telling teachers what and how to teach, there are isolated cases of continuing success, and there are ways of measuring those successes. Chapter 6 "Is it Magic, Miracles, or Motivation?" points out an individual example of high achievement. Year after year, I have seen my classes gain an average of one or two stanine points in standardized math tests. Stanine points are used by school districts to evaluate students' progress. Stanine levels go from one to nine. Five tends to be the average score expected for grade-level work, while stanines above five reflect higher than average achievement on a particular test. Students who get stanines of eight or nine are now usually considered to be in the high-achievement classification.

Whether the class I taught was a fifth-grade bilingual class in the eighties, a multigraded class of high-I.Q. students in the seventies, a multicultural, multilanguage fifth–sixth-grade class with a mixture of special education students as well as a cluster of bright students in the nineties, or just an average class of fifth graders (which in Los Angeles meant a cluster of English as a second language [ESL] students), they continued as a group to show remarkable improvement on standardized tests over the previous year's scores. I suspect that the amazing scores can be attributed to the sense of security that I arranged in the classroom as well as clear, consistent guidelines and high expectations for the students.

It is scary to realize that years have passed since the Reagan administration released its "Nation at Risk" report, and we still do not have agreed-upon standards and values for our school system. That report's assertion that "if an unfriendly foreign power had attempted to impose on America the mediocre educational performance that exists today, we might well have viewed it as an act of war" is just as true today, in the new millennium, as it was when written in the eighties.

Reflecting back on how teachers had been trained to teach and what they should expect students to learn at a certain grade level, one realizes that four or five decades ago most teachers were not given any specific standards. Teachers started teaching kindergarten in the fifties only knowing that the five-year-olds should learn the subject matter that their training teacher had shown them during their few months with her. As I taught my first kindergarten class, I kept wondering what they would be required to know the next year. On my own I investigated the first-grade program at my school to see what I should do to prepare my five-year-olds. Preparing my class for the next grade became my theme song as there was not any written, clearly defined statement as to what we teachers were supposed to achieve with the students the year they were under our supervision. There was only a vaguely expressed principle that the students were to be socialized.

It was not until the seventies that teachers first received from the Los Angeles Unified School District (LAUSD) an itemized listing of achievement standards for students at each grade level. In 1975 the *Elementary School Curriculum: Guidelines for Instruction* was distributed to schools and teachers. I congratulate the district on this forward step. Other districts in Southern California had not given their teachers an outline as to what they were expected to teach at each grade. The listing in Los Angeles's guide showed at what grade a specific concept was first introduced, then reviewed, and at what grade it was to be tested.

This was a valuable asset to teachers. Fellow teachers would feel at a loss when they moved out of the area and found that their new district did not give them any guidelines. If they were teaching a grade level that was new to them, they would then call an LAUSD teacher and ask for information from the Los Angeles guide. Teachers want guidelines. It is not fair to students if one grade keeps repeating concepts without teaching new material. There was and is an obvious need for a systematic schedule of what skills should be taught and when they should appear in the curriculum.

In the seventies, five-year-olds were not tested, but grades one to six were tested on the achievement goals. The goals may not have been perfect, but they were there for everyone to see, to read, and to hold as an objective to be reached. Parents, as well as teachers, could easily identify what material was to be mastered.

Unfortunately, those grade-level goals, which were clearly understood and quickly tested by using multiple-choice-type questions, are now considered old-fashioned. The newer updated manual for the nineties identified broad-based general concepts rather than specific ones. The concepts are so ephemeral that one can only paraphrase what is to be done in fifth-grade history by saying the students are supposed to be aware of a multicultural society, the differences and similarities. In English they are to have the opportunity to write as often as possible. Work in progress is to be discussed with a partner.

This is a vastly different approach than the specific to-be-tested concepts at each grade level that was seen in the first curriculum guide. Ideally, both types of goals should be included. A good fifth-grade class can develop an awareness of the interrelationships between the European cultures and the Native American cultures of the fifteenth century after they have read and understood what happened in trade, commerce, and agriculture following Christopher Columbus's voyage.

Parents, wanting some kind of guideline in the nineties, told me that they were happy to be able to see the index of the reading workbook.

The index itemized the reading skills the students should have been studying, but the workbook had to stay at school in the students' desks. Many parents are incredibly thankful to get their hands on some kind of help. It makes it possible for the parents and teacher to work as a team. What the teacher is teaching their child should not have to be a mystery.

There is no question in my mind that striving to achieve well-defined, reachable goals is not only commendable, it is necessary, for it brings great satisfaction and a sense of empowerment to the children who have had the opportunity to learn and grow in a secure environment. I believe that the academic success of students should be a national success story. But first, Americans must agree on the values of effort and perseverance. We must not be afraid to draw up national goals and academic standards for our country.

PART 2

There is a need for today's students to have a sense of community. A feeling of belonging can be established in the classroom. The following chapters tell about techniques that will lead to a sense of community.

The changes that American society went through during the last half of the twentieth century, and how those cultural upheavals affected the school system, are explained and examples are given.

7

THE CLASSROOM AS A COMMUNITY

Family and social structure in the United States were much different in the fifties. As one continues to watch the dissolution, decade after decade, of many of our social structures, especially those desperately needed by growing children, a good teacher realizes how much today's child, the child of the new millennium, needs a sense of community. Youngsters need a place where they can feel safe and secure to be themselves, while exhibiting a social sense that includes the values of *respect*, *responsibility*, *consideration*, and *sensitivity*. There needs to be a sense of community within the classroom. That can be consciously promoted through the use of several strategies. Very often a teacher's goals will intersect with each other.

Most teachers find it difficult to increase students' vocabulary development. Remembering that this is the television generation and much communication is received passively, it is wise to devise a scheme to make learning new vocabulary words meaningful and fun at the same time. It has to be done at school. Anytime you want to see academic success from students, you have to make sure they have time to do the work at school. Experience shows that they learn much more at school than at home. I suspect parents' overburdened schedules and lack of motivation cause this problem.

So a device to promote vocabulary can also further a feeling of community. Cooperative groups can compete against each other to get the highest score on a version of charades. First, develop the groups. A teacher should not do this until he or she has been with the students for several weeks. Use good judgment to see who would profit by being placed in a leadership position and at the same time not be overburdened, or suffer from classmates' jealousies. You need to know each student's academic ability in order to make up a number of groups of equal size that will be fairly competitive with each other. This means that after you have made up the six groups of five to six students each (it won't always be exactly equal), you call the designated leaders aside and talk to them separately.

Explain that each group has been selected carefully and is equal, meaning that each set has students who find schoolwork easy, some who find it so-so, and some who find it very difficult. Each team is to have a leader, chosen because he or she has exhibited leadership qualities in the classroom and on the playground. Give them the names of the members of their groups and assign a number to each group (1–6).

After that, call upon another set of students, one for each group, who have a different role in the group. They are to be called the observers. Whereas the leader's purpose is to be goal oriented and achieve whatever task the teacher devises, the observers are to pay attention to the individuals on each team. Their job is to promote or to solicit participation from any student who doesn't immediately feel comfortable in adding to the discussions.

These teams can be together for half the year with the same members and roles. The second half of the year, revise the groups using the same process. New students can then be given the leadership roles. Some might be new to the school or have just recently shown that they will excel in the role of leader and are usually eager to have that opportunity.

These groups foster a sense of team unity. It is a type of competition where every person's ability helps the group. Therefore, it is up to the leader to promote an atmosphere that helps everyone learn what needs to be learned. This should also be explained to the leaders privately. It is fun to watch how seriously they will address their roles and responsibilities. It is an important and worthwhile job for them to undertake.

Now, your task is to develop that vocabulary. All groups are given the same list of twenty words from their recent studies that need to be understood thoroughly and mastered. In each team the leader will assume the responsibility of dividing up the task: to first define the words, then memorize the meanings, and finally decide how to indicate that word to their group. The words can be acted out. What fun it is to watch them act out the word *sauntering*. Or the word can be drawn on the chalkboard. The obvious simplicity of writing *100* for century is one of the few simple examples. Both creativity and competition are fostered while team members are learning to be cooperative with each other.

When you determine that enough time for learning has taken place, put the twenty words, each on a small slip of paper, into a big black top hat, stir them up, and call on Group 1. All the groups will be called upon, in order, one after the other. It is the group leader's job to tell each group member that it is his or her turn. The leaders have to remember who has been given a turn and make sure everyone has a turn, including themselves. Discuss with them privately the importance of not making anyone feel that they are always first or always last. They can devise different ways to do this fairly. Not every leader will use the same process.

When each group member comes to the front of the room where you stand with the hat, dramatically pull out a slip and hold it so only the team member can read it. The student's job is then to show the class what the word is through the use of pantomime or a drawing. This often develops a strong sense of the meaning of the word. They can even discern subtle differences between the words *enclose* and *insert*.

No other group can help with the word or they will be cheating themselves. However, they will see a similar or different representation of the word and be learning with a fun repetitive drill the whole time. If a group guesses the word correctly, they get a point. Then, it is the next group's turn. If the word isn't guessed, the answer needs to be given by you. Each group always gets a fresh word. This means that no group is lording it over another group other than in the accumulated score. It is good to advise the groups that if an adult comes in to ask what they are doing having so much fun, they need to explain that they are not playing a game, but that they are studying their vocabulary words.

The teacher's own test, each year, is to see if he or she has chosen groups correctly. If the scores are very even, you have done your job. Often it is fine. If not, talk privately to the leaders to discuss how to make it more competitive. Sometimes, a winning leader can join another group for a session, and that seems to work without any bad feelings.

There is a sense of involvement and dependence on the group. A warm, proud awareness of the group develops. Students new to the class or school are given lots of encouragement. Shouts of "We know you know it," "It's O.K., you're doing fine," and "You can do it" are common. There is much cheering when the word is discovered. If a student's group misses out on a point because of their inability, the leader should work with them as a group to learn it. If it is the inability of a particular student, the whole group can reinforce the meaning of the word and remind the student how to do it. This is to be done in a sensitive, considerate way, as that is the only way they should ever be allowed to proceed, and they should be very aware of their teacher's feelings on the subject. Make it clear that it is tough to get up in front of your friends, let alone a bunch of strangers. Encouragement is accepted; making fun of someone or putting down a member of the group is inexcusable. How exciting it is to see that the students can learn with ease and speed, and that they have the opportunity of working cooperatively with a group. They now have a group to depend upon, a group that accepts them and their efforts.

So, a teacher sneakily develops a strong sense of belonging, a sense of community, a sense of having a group to call one's own and that helps and appreciates them. At the same time the teacher gets vocabulary taught all during the time the students think they are having fun. A good teacher needs to prove to herself or himself that this technique works. After several weeks have passed, the students should get a written test on forty to eighty vocabulary words, and you can then evaluate whether they have learned and retained the new words. It works!

The role of leadership is more clearly understood by those who have that task. It is interesting to see how much they learn about themselves and others by giving leadership to their group. You can often overhear the group of leaders discussing, by themselves, the difficulties or successes they had experienced. Once many of these students have performed in leadership roles, they continue to be leaders as they advance to higher grade levels. It is satisfying to see such strong leadership evidence itself in middle school and high school.

These same groups can be used in other subject areas as study groups. One day's task might be to study a new chapter in history together. Most teachers will find it exciting to listen to the discussions as the students paraphrase the text, show examples, and discuss and argue their points. A different day might find them solving a logic or critical thinking problem that needs everyone's help and input. One type of favorite puzzle, in conjunction with an aerodynamics lesson that focuses on Bernoulli's principle, is to see which group can first solve the age-old problem of the farmer transporting his fox, grain, and chicken in a small boat across a river. Change the circumstances to fit the science lesson, so that the groups need to solve how the pilot of an ultralight flying machine would transport each item. The constraint is that the items cannot be left together unattended as the fox might eat the chicken, and the chicken might eat the grain. The pilot can only take one thing at a time, because the plane can only carry a certain amount of weight.

During the cooperative group work, students have the opportunity to become aware of their own particular talents as they relate to working with others. Let's imagine one of the leaders. Let's assume that he has shown exceptional talent as a leader. You might become curious to see how he will participate as a regular group member when it is time to switch positions of responsibility.

Some do seem to be born leaders. They also have the ability to wait and see if others can lead. While watching the exceptional leader, you might see her or him wait patiently as a new student tries to get the group organized. Time goes by, and the group has not started to work on the task. The waiting leader's body language will show tension, and then, finally, a resigned look will appear on his or her face, as though he or she was saying, "Oh well, it might be best if I stepped in now and helped them out." The leader will then subtly and quietly direct the group to the task at hand, and progress will be made. Some teachers will want to stay in contact and see how this student continues to use his or her talent. It is not unusual to find that this type of student will hold a student body office in secondary school.

Without opportunities at an early age to take the role of leadership, many students might not know how well they can perform in that capacity. It is wonderful to have the advantage of trying out these new adventures in a safe environment.

8

CLASS PLAYS PROMOTE A SENSE OF COMMUNITY

Putting on a play for the rest of the school promotes a feeling of unity within a class. As an example, imagine a class of thirty-six fifth graders. Select a play that not only has starring roles with much dialogue and acting, but also has some type of chorus or group recital work. In order to have every class member involved, have those who are not main characters seated at all times on stage as a chorus. Their lines can be spoken together. If a member of that group gets stage fright, it will not seem devastating. Everyone in the class should understand that they can all be on stage, have a part, and take a bow at the end before a large auditorium audience of students, teachers, principal, and parents.

However, not all plays are written for a cast of three dozen thespians. In one particular play, a teacher might develop a set that needs students to hold either a flower or an onion on a bulletin board–sized poster. On cue, they would come into the audience area in a choreographed manner. Most will be astonished at how many students will want one of these parts. All the boys as well as the girls will want to participate. No one will laugh at the idea. It becomes obvious just how important it is to students to be in their class play. There will be lots of volunteers for parts a teacher writes himself or herself in order to accommodate everyone.

It does help to present a rationale to them as to why their part is integral to the play. A good teacher also realizes how much security there is for them to be surrounded by others doing the same thing. These will be students who do not want a starring role for one reason or another. Enough stars do emerge, however, to stage two or three performances, each with a different starring cast.

Dignity is of the utmost importance to students. Trying out for a play for the first time can be very scary. The teacher's task is to alleviate the scariness and keep the students' sense of personal dignity intact while they are auditioning. This can be done by holding individual auditions in a hallway or private space, hopefully keeping an eye on the classroom at the same time that the aspiring thespian is auditioning in privacy. It is important to make it clear to those who are trying out that you are looking for three abilities. They must be able to memorize the part, project their voice in order to be heard, and "act" the lines.

Everyone who wants a speaking part should be allowed to audition. This sometimes takes several days. The teacher should announce his or her decision to each aspirant privately. Those who do not win the audition can have the opportunity to be understudies. If students just like the idea of being in a play, but do not have the tenacity to learn lines, they are spared the discomfort of standing in front of the class during an audition while it is discovered that they did not know the lines well enough to star. Since their dignity is intact, they can find other ways to participate in the play. It is good to listen to all their ideas and to try to fit them into the production.

This brings the class together in an exciting, worthwhile project in which they are all involved. The fact that it isn't easy and is scary gives them a good sense of their cooperative accomplishment. Some might bring costumes or make them for others. A few will act as drama coaches, and one or two will find the courage to play the piano for the onion/flower chorus. You can see these young people develop a satisfying sense of togetherness by participating in this project. It is a satisfaction based on helping each other to achieve their best.

This is also another opportunity for the teacher to show boys and girls that he or she will not ask them to do anything that would embarrass them or cause them undue discomfort. Trust and security allow them to feel free to try out new ideas. The children can feel comfortable, as no one will harass them for being themselves.

9

A SENSE OF COMMUNITY
THROUGH POETRY

Poetry can become another vehicle for establishing a sense of classroom community. Every fall the students memorize most of "What Is Black?" by Mary O'Neill. Later in the year they might memorize Robert Frost's "Walking through the Woods" or Henry Wadsworth Longfellow's "Paul Revere's Ride." Reciting the poem in front of the class by themselves can be part of their oral language grade. It is necessary to have all the children use the same poem in order to give the boys and girls a sense of security so that the poem they have to recite will not be thought of as silly or strange. In particular "Paul Revere's Ride" has a great beat to it. It can almost be chanted, and the students love practicing it daily.

A teacher needs to be careful when grading time comes to choose a row of children that appears to have self-assured boys and girls in it as the group to perform the first day. Call their names, one at time, in the order in which they sit in the row. Call on a different group each day. They should know a week ahead of time when they will have to recite. The last row to be called on should be the group with students who might be more fearful about getting up and performing for perhaps the first time in their lives. This gives them several more days before they have to perform. During that time, they can keep working on the poem as others perform. It works.

Everyone takes their turn to get up and recite. When they have finished, they should receive a big round of applause from the rest of the
class. It becomes almost like a rite of passage. You can imagine by
watching their body language that they were thinking, "I did it. I was
brave. I'm a part of the group." It seems as though they are passing
through a test of acceptance, a feeling of ritual that is missing in today's
anonymous society.

Their memory of these poems can be used to continue their sense of
classroom community when they are part of a larger group, as when they
are in the school auditorium for a program and the guest performer has
not yet arrived. Everyone gets bored and restless waiting around. Quite
often there will be about six other classes in the auditorium. Quietly ask
the class if they remember "What Is Black?" As they nod affirmatively,
say, "One, two, go!" and all will belt it out with much glee. It can be their
special time to perform extemporaneously as a class. They will be developing their sense of group pride while having fun and using up some
of the boring time spent waiting around for the performer to arrive.

10

THE CLASSROOM AS A SAFE REFUGE

Today's teachers are becoming aware that for some of their students, school is their one safe retreat. Coming in early in the morning, or asking to see their teacher privately in the hall or at recess, they will unload their fears and concerns. Some are overburdened with parental conflict at home. Others have parents who have just lost their jobs or parents who are in jail. A few have siblings who terrorize them with violence. These children desperately need the sense of security and comfort that the classroom, as a community, gives them to survive through the day. School, for them, is a refuge.

Imagine the child who comes to school in the morning feeling upset about her parents shouting at her and blaming her for many small infractions. She finds it hard to concentrate on her work. After she tells her teacher what is troubling her, the teacher can help somewhat by listening, being sympathetic, and allowing her to write in a journal about the problems her parents are having as they consider getting a divorce. This child can then be given the opportunity to keep the journal in a locked closet in the classroom. This validates her feelings and concerns and allows her to feel relaxed enough to do her schoolwork.

A refuge offers security to expand one's talents. Students in the late seventies who were bright were classified as mentally gifted minors

(MGM). Many of these very young people knew the answers to questions being asked but could not verbalize their thoughts when called upon in class. Some days it reminded one of *Welcome Back Kotter*. That television series had shown students who raised their waving hands eagerly, but when called upon, no words came out, just a few guttural sounds. Two activities to help these bright children become more comfortable in formulating their thoughts are debates and "expert reports."

Debate subjects can evolve as a homework project. Students can discuss likely subjects for debate with their parents and make a list to present to the class. From these lists, the teacher gleans enough subjects so that everyone in the class will have an opportunity to argue a concept. Parents love to participate, and this is an easy way for them to be involved without too much time sacrificed.

The teacher needs to carefully select each pair of students who will challenge each other. It is important that they are equal in ability in order to avoid any unnecessary embarrassment. As much choice as possible is given to students to engage in verbal conflict on their own subject. Research time needs to be allotted, and information as to how a debate is run needs to be taught. The debates are a highlight. Rebuttals prompt the ability to speak extemporaneously and well.

Now that the students have the security of knowing they can recite poetry in front of the class, and debate, the teacher has the opportunity to enrich their ability to research and discuss ideas in front of a group. It is so difficult to be called upon, in secondary schools or in one's career, to perform in this manner if one hasn't had previous experience.

An expert report is basically a research project on a subject decided upon by the student. Many times children are asked to become knowledgeable in areas that have little interest for them. It should be understood that the teacher has veto power over their choice of a theme. Mainly this is to help a boy or girl select a subject that is narrow enough. "Continents" or "Space" is too broad. One also needs to veto an expert report on Charles Manson. It is important to be willing to have a student investigate an area that interests him or her, but you must withhold permission on subjects that are not considered educational to the child or those listening to the report.

Parents and students should be advised of this study requirement early on in the school year. Many lessons need to be taught showing how to organize ideas, take notes and research, and write a bibliography. The report is to be first researched and written. Then it is turned in to the teacher for comments and approval. After the report is returned, a time needs to be assigned for the oral presentation, which is the only grade the student will receive for all this work. The writing process is understood by the boys and girls to be part of the process of learning and organizing material for a presentation.

Many local librarians tell how aghast they are at the number of parents who are doing their children's homework. The adults are writing and researching a topic for their child. Too often written reports just become the rephrasing of a lot of material with very little awareness of what the subject is really about. This does not happen with expert reports!

The student's task is to stand in front of the class and talk like an expert. These presentations are similar to college lectures. A student might have a slide presentation from a family trip that shows the dolphins she was talking about. Since audiovisual aids, including videotapes or slides, can be used, these classroom assignments often turn into great parent–child projects.

Another child might give an oral presentation on pizza with accompanying videotape showing his interview with the manager of a local pizzeria. The excitement of this forty-minute presentation is heightened when you know that this is a student who has trouble in school academically and is tutored privately every day. No one in the class, including the teacher, will know as much about pizza as the student expert does.

Imagine a special education student who gives her presentation on astronauts and their training, including the history of the program. As she stands in front of her classmates comfortably discussing all she knows about astronauts, her teacher will have trouble remembering that this is the student who goes to the Resource Room every day as her academic tests from the previous years showed that she was a low achiever. This can be her time to shine and amaze all. She will receive tumultuous applause after her forty-five-minute presentation.

The students' sense of security in their classroom community allows them to understand each other's strengths and weaknesses, and they will be delighted to see one of their group who has not always been successful show a surprising talent. The praise from classmates will continue as the students leave the room to go to recess or lunch.

The ability to speak in front of others can be carried forward one more step. If a class is involved with a younger age group as "special friends," they will have the opportunity to go to that classroom and give their expert report. There is also another opportunity. Students who choose to have the additional experience can go to the next lower grade classrooms to present their reports. These younger students are then prepared the next year when you, their new teacher, start to discuss expert reports.

The students who go to other classes will come back and report to their own class what they, as a guest lecturer, have experienced. It is interesting to see how much they value a quiet, responsive audience. They have become used to that in their own room. Because they feel a sense of mastery from giving their report in their own room, they can deliver their report even when another class is not well-behaved. However, the students will be rather amazed and somewhat annoyed that all classes do not give the kind of attention to the speaker that their own class gives as a common courtesy.

Good audience response in their own room requires that the teacher monitors anyone who is playing with a pencil, paper, or book. Discuss what good audience behavior and courtesy is and tell them that you will be watching to see that it takes place. A safe refuge, then, is one where no one will make fun of you, you will be encouraged, and your efforts will be appreciated. It is a place where one can grow and expand one's talents.

When there is this safety, the feeling of community can do much in giving one a good sense of pride, not only in one's own achievements, but in the accomplishments of the group as well. I am describing a community that has the shared values of *responsibility*, *respect*, *consideration*, and *sensitivity*. It can be a thrill to realize that after several years in middle school, students still have a special feeling about their experience in your class, an experience that was extraordinary because of the added feeling of community that you develop year after year.

❶❶

THE CLASSROOM FROM THE FIFTIES THROUGH THE NINETIES

During the fifties one could casually mention to a mother picking up her son that his behavior had been somewhat errant that day. Presto! Since families in the fifties were a major social agency, the boy changed his behavior simply and easily. Hard to believe that ever happened, but it did. I know because I was there. Those were the days when mothers came to school in tennis outfits to pick up their children.

The sixties brought some changes. Now barefoot moms picked up their sons and daughters. Some families spoke English as a second language. Drugs and their use became part of the environment. One day a teenage girl walked into the school's kindergarten room with her blouse opened from top to bottom, exposing lots of bare skin. After what seemed like a long time, the teacher safely dismissed the class and addressed the problem of this unknown high school girl who appeared stoned and very out of it. Finally getting her home phone number, the office personnel and teacher tried in vain to get her family to come pick her up. The staff did not think she was safe walking around in that state of undressed blissfulness, but their concern was not felt by her relatives. In the sixties a mother stole the kindergarten class's flowers out of their garden plot. Regardless of how one viewed "flower children," that really ticked that teacher off.

Most teachers are taught many valuable lessons by the children in their classes. Most classes are eager to teach their teacher new ways to motivate and challenge them. It can be a great training experience as one moves through various elementary schools teaching different grade levels and children with varied needs. One lesson is that a child, at the age of five, can learn to read if you let him roll over and over on the rug as he holds onto his book reading out loud. A good teacher discovers that one group of kindergarten children wants to learn to read up to the second-grade level, while another group needs to study basic vocabulary words such as *nose, mouth, hair,* etc., in English. These children can enjoy being in a group that has similar tasks while others concentrate on different areas of the curriculum.

Another child can teach that what works with groups does not always work when a child feels isolated. Imagine a kindergarten child who is ready to read at a plateau above anyone else. There are not any other students at his advanced level in that particular kindergarten class. A teacher might think it would be just dandy to let him read for fifteen or twenty minutes with a first-grade class in a room close by. No way! That child might not perform in the other class and might not show any interest at all in leaving his own classroom, even though there is a higher level of enrichment available. It might be a fellow classmate's influence that is partly to blame. This little boy might have quite a crush on a little girl and does not intend to be out of her sight. Here is another lesson that the children can teach us.

The seventies brought a new wave of immigrants to the schools. Vietnamese students were introduced. The beginning of a truly multicultural community was being established. Suddenly English as a second language and bilingual education stepped in as new methods. Paperwork amassed around these students' files as each new category or teaching method needed additional assessment and testing. Teachers who progressed to teaching the upper elementary grades were delighted to realize that all the talk of sheltered English and English as a second language was simply the same language development approach any good kindergarten teacher used in order to be successful.

Every teacher knows by observing children's logic and critical thinking skills that even if a student does not have English language fluency, he or she can be quite smart. Chess becomes a good technique to help

the English-speaking students realize that those who know other languages as their primary tongue can compete successfully. This promotes
a good feeling of camaraderie, as well as mutual respect. After teaching
chess to the class as a whole, allow them to play once a week on "Fabulous Friday." Fabulous Friday can be a day when all subjects are taught,
but they are presented in different, offbeat ways. Chess can be the math
lesson on Friday, and competition can become keen. At the end of the
year, the students can compete among themselves to win the chess tro-
phy the teacher has bought as a prize. It can be a hard-fought competition with a high interest level. Studying new strategies with books the
teacher has made available can be enjoyed by the students at home and
in class.

One of the highlights of this seventies period was the development of
a multigraded class of students who had been designated through testing as MGMs. The grade levels encompassed second through sixth. It
was this multicultural group that competed regionally in a chess tourna-
ment. Los Angeles sometimes holds an annual student chess competition for the western and eastern halves of the city. The competition is
usually run as a professional match on a Saturday. The community feeling in the multigraded class was enhanced as students helped each other
prepare for the competition, and parents arranged transportation via car
pools for all who participated. Not only did that class win the competition for the Western Division of Los Angeles, but the top player and
first-place winner was one of the Vietnamese girls. How exciting that experience was for the class! The trophies were proudly exhibited in the
room during Open House that spring.

Honesty and integrity must be an integral part of any teacher's program and should be evidenced in many daily events. Even though the
students were overjoyed at their chess prowess, they cheerfully con-
fessed to admirers that they had probably won first place in the city because they had more players competing than any other school. Their
teacher could be pleased with their honest assessment of the situation.
Additionally, she could be happy to see their awareness that a group
could have merit in what they did together.

The eighties appeared, and suddenly even upper-middle-class children seemed to be "orphans." "Orphans" in the sense that their outside
world had become so violent and unfriendly in many instances that

these boys and girls were told to stay at home, have friends walk with them on their way to and from school, and watch out for strangers. That was the decade when some students were fearfully discussing which of them had personally known the girl who had been kidnapped and killed in their northwest hillside community of Los Angeles.

It was hard for a teacher to get the class's attention one Monday after spring break when a heated discussion raged over whether a man had been killed by a gun or a machete. This was the main topic of attention in a middle- to upper-middle-class city in Southern California. Realizing that this topic was of more immediate interest than the planned fifth-grade lesson, the teacher monitored their discussion. She was surprised at the involvement of one of her students, who told how his mother wouldn't allow him to get on his bicycle to chase the murderer. Arguments were finally resolved when it was discovered that there had actually been two homicides Easter Sunday, one machete death and one gun death.

The nineties saw children who often came to school after taking care of their parents. They had to assume the role of the responsible adult as their parents were having so much trouble in their own life that they could not manage. Media coverage often centers on how much neglect and abuse is actually going on in our families. *Dysfunctional* is now a mainstream word. The word is abstract, but the lack of family security and the absence of time and interest that is available to be invested in children present a dreadful social situation.

As a teacher, you are legally mandated to report physical abuse cases. When possible abuse cases arise, you must investigate and call the local school authorities. The police are often called after school authorities have reviewed the case. Then the student can be taken with any siblings to the police station, and the parents are notified to not pick up the children at school that day. At one school, an abused child was taken by officers to the police station because of the welts on her legs. The bruises and abrasions were the result of a beating because she did not flush the toilet at her home.

Imagine finding yourself in the office as acting principal. You look out the office window at the precise moment that a mother is dragging a boy off the school grounds. This mother felt that the boy had said something nasty or derogatory to her daughter, and as she dragged him along with her she castigated and threatened him. Once again, information on how to handle situations like this was not usually part of the curriculum in all those education classes most of us took. Acting on instinct, you might race out of the office thinking how dreadful it would be for the boy if you grabbed his other arm and then had a tug of war with him in the middle. Often there is not enough time to give the office staff any directions other than to alert them to the situation. Your feet and mind are racing together. This woman outweighs you by a large number of pounds. Turn on that acting skill that is such an important part of the job. Stopping right in front of her with a huge smile, say, "Good Morning Mrs. Anymother! How are you today?" Not expecting this response she momentarily loosens her grip, and you shout, "Run!" Later, after the parent of the child who had been grabbed by Mrs. Anymother goes to court with the case, you are called as a witness. It is then that you discover from a court official that using foul language and threatening someone is considered assault. That was an eighties lesson.

In the nineties, at a different upper-middle-class school, you might momentarily be called out of your fifth-grade class to fulfill the role of acting principal. It could be a bomb scare. It seems that many acting principals have never been given information as to proper procedure for bomb scares. Maybe colleges think teachers are just supposed to teach. With the help of an outstanding office staff and plant manager, you secure the school, keep the students in safe areas, and alert the teachers. Run to all the rooms but whisper the scary information to the teachers to alleviate a panic situation as all wait for the police. Fortunately it is usually a hoax. Unfortunately, the perpetrator usually isn't discovered.

Violence on the streets is now commonplace. This was brought home to one teacher when her student told her how happy she was that she had not been shot. This teacher had asked her to walk around the perimeter of the inside of the school grounds during physical education as she didn't like to participate in sports. She would often just stand dreamily at the volleyball court, putting herself and others in jeopardy while the action of the game was in progress. She had not been able to keep up with the other students on a recent one-mile walk to an orientation meeting at the local middle school.

The student told this to the teacher while she was walking around the area with her. It was a good private time for children to relate a concern to her. Quite often part of the physical education period is not only the time to teach skills, but also a time to listen and counsel on a one-to-one basis. That teacher had kept an eye on the girl at all times and thought she was perfectly safe, getting some of the physical fitness training that is part of the fifth-grade curriculum. When it was time to go back to the room, the girl let her know that she had been worried that someone on the main street next to the school and playground might have shot her. Drive-by-shooting incidents had been in the news all that year. That was the last time that teacher used that area for her, or anyone else, to walk.

This ten-year-old girl's fearfulness can be understood by looking at the cover of the September 1993 issue of *The New Yorker*. With a yellow school bus in the background, the drawing on the cover shows young children, about the age of first or second graders, on their way to school carrying machine guns and rifles in one hand, lunch pails in the other.

12

FROM SPUTNIK TO TOMATO SEEDS FROM SPACE

In the fifties, there was a strong awareness that Sputnik, the orbiting Russian spacecraft, was making an impression on Americans that education, especially science and math, assumed a place of prime national importance. This was also the post–World War II era, when globally many nations were becoming interested in improving their educational systems.

As a woman, it was an exciting time to have a career. Not every woman was looking for a profession at that time. Most of my friends had opted to marry and have children. I opted for a husband, a son, and a career.

This was the era when parents were told that they would ruin their children if they tried to teach them to read. Supposedly, only teachers and the educational system knew the magic and intricacies of properly teaching boys and girls to read. Some teachers chose to believe the famous anthropologist of that era, Margaret Mead, when she pointed out that if parents were literate they should be able to teach their children to read. That made sense to many new young teachers. They were happy to have parental involvement available, even though the teacher was still considered the expert, and their opinion carried a lot of weight. It is ironic to realize in this new millennium that many, if not most, parents prefer to pay to have a tutor help their child learn a difficult subject or catch up on some material. I suspect that money is more abundant than time.

Teaching in the late nineties meant teaching during an era of exciting space development. In the sixties, American astronauts went to the moon, and the landing was seen nationally on television. By the mid-nineties space shuttles had become more common, and some teachers had tomato seeds from NASA for their fifth graders' research project.

Unfortunately, the United States no longer had the unity and purpose of the fifties. The civil rights causes in the sixties, the Vietnam War, and the Cold War all had a disrupting effect on national unity and purpose. Churches, families, and scout troops were no longer unifying social structures. That meant that the teacher took over many of the roles these now somewhat dormant social institutions had covered. Voids do have a way of getting filled. Good teachers have added lessons about values, self-discipline, manners, showering, laundering, anger control, and drug education to their plans. The teacher's role has increased to that of a substitute parent and counselor. Unfortunately, the six-hour school day has not increased to allow time for all the additional duties. Teachers, as well as the rest of the population, are feeling overwhelmed with ill-defined tasks that took more than the allotted time.

The change was slow in developing. That made it harder to be aware of all the ramifications. Imagine a teacher preparing to go on a leave of absence for the first time. She was not prepared for the distress of one of her fifth-grade students when she departed from the classroom one day in February to go on her sabbatical. One of her ten-year-olds accompanied her as she walked to the faculty parking lot. When they got there, he demanded a hug and held onto her arm, impeding her leaving. It took a while before his grip relaxed, and she was in her car and on her way. This boy, a special education student, had never shown such a connection to her before. She was suddenly overwhelmed with the realization that she had caused him to feel abandoned. It was a painful experience.

Looking back over her memories, she was aware that this was a new reaction from children. In previous decades, parents had been there for the children, and teachers were simply a part of the educational process. Now as teachers have taken over some of the needed parental roles, our physical presence or lack of it has a whole new implication for the students. And that is a frightening and thought-provoking issue.

PART 3

The chapters on special programs (bilingual education and classes for gifted students) show how the students in them were competing and achieving in the last half of the twentieth century.

There is also an overview of the history of education and a presentation of the classroom teacher's image on television.

13

WHICH CAME FIRST: PUBLIC EDUCATION OR THE PROBLEMS AND CONTROVERSY?

How did it all begin? Realizing that public education in the United States is not yet two hundred years old helps clear up some of the questions as to why we are still arguing so much about the pros and cons of how it should be done. Should we have programs for the exceptional child? What is the best way to organize and plan for gifted students? Is it better to mandate special classes for bilingual boys and girls? What should be done for the physically, mentally, and emotionally handicapped? What is the best and most efficient program for a specific group, and how is it going to be financed?

The above questions are closely interrelated with the well-being of the United States. We live, more and more, in a global society. To know how we, as Americans, can best survive, it is profitable to take a look at history in order to see how and why the educational system that we now have was initiated.

Public education in America seems to have developed between the years 1828 and 1865. This was a period of industrialization, immigration, urbanization, humanitarianism, and technology. The Westward Movement had begun, and there was an interest in the nature of man and the nature of children. Geographically, different parts of the country at that time were developing dissimilar lifestyles. The people in the West were busy in their independence and settling of new lands and building of homes. The South was caught up in slavery as an economical way to bring in the huge, profitable cotton harvests. The Northeast was experiencing industrialization. The domestic manufacturing in village homes and workshops was moving to factory towns. Cotton from the South was milled in the North. Besides the effect of Eli Whitney's cotton gin, there was the Goulding condenser, which transferred filaments of wool to different machines, and there was the sewing machine.

It is said that in 1820 about $8 million came from the production of cloth in northern states' wool and cotton mills. In 1830, ten years later, the amount was about $58 million, and in 1860 it was $330 million. In addition to the manufacturing increases, there were great strides being made in the effectiveness of mass transportation. There was the steamboat and Stephenson's locomotive. The Erie Canal was completed in 1825, and around 1829 the first steam engines were used on American railroads. This increased the movements of people and goods to the West and expanded the national market. The invention of the telegraph increased the connections between both people and areas.

It was a time of many technological advances. The craftsmanship that previously produced a shoe, a piece of cloth, a rifle, or a watch was being taken over by machines. Labor became organized. Around 1833, the New England Association of Farmers, Mechanics, and Other Working Men claimed that two-fifths of factory workers in New England were children between the ages of seven and sixteen who toiled fourteen hours daily, six days a week. The working conditions were often dangerous, the hours long, the work tedious, and the pay minimal. It seems that these factors, plus the hopelessness of ever rising above this poverty level, led to the emergence of a school-minded working class in the northern cities.

At the same time that the above changes were taking place in America, Europe's poor economic situation resulted in a large influx of immigrants to the United States from Ireland, Germany, England, and the Scandinavian countries. The influx of new settlers that started in 1825 with about 10,000 immigrants reached a total of about 215,000 in 1854. Many of these new arrivals were impoverished before they boarded the boat to come to America. As they disembarked from their ships in the harbors of the northeastern states, they did not have enough money to travel to the West or to buy property in the South. So, they stayed close to where they had first stepped upon American soil, and they became the residents and workers in the newly industrialized urban areas.

Old religious differences promoted new arguments, and the immigrants were held responsible for the increase in crime. There were fears that the new arrivals would not assimilate into American society. Educational reformers used the ferment caused by the wave of foreigners to further their cause. They rallied their forces around the idea that the common school, more than any other social institution, would help to "Americanize" the outsiders. There was the hope that public education would check the onrush of social upheaval by teaching the new arrivals the responsibilities of citizenship. Schools were to elevate the masses from lives of squalor and poverty by widening their economic opportunities and by training them in proper social habits. At the very least, it was hoped that a respect for law and authority would be instilled.

Now, almost two hundred years later, as we find ourselves in a new millennium, we can be impressed that so many people have received an outstanding education and preparation for their adult life. Even though schools have not been perfect, and they can be better, it helps when we look at the background. There are startling similarities between what we experienced in twentieth-century American life and what we read about how people in our country lived in the nineteenth century. About a hundred years ago, the general populace may have felt that the economic, ecclesiastical, and political roles that had been established by traditional Puritan virtues were no longer as applicable. It seemed that the decline of church discipline and social influence made it an unreliable institution for instructing children in their social obligations.

Horace Mann's rallying cry as the "father of public education" seemed to be asking voters if they agreed that pernicious family and social influences undermined the proper training of children. Public education was seen, by some, as a form of social insurance. In 1841, as he championed the benefits of public education, Mann said, "Other social organizations are curative and remedial, but the common school is a preventive and an antidote." He felt schools would be efficient in doing away with nine-tenths of the crime. He expected that rational hopes in respect to the future would brighten when his plan was endorsed.

The relationship between industrialization, urbanism, and immigration led to social unrest and disorder. A solution was seen in the development of the public school. A replacement was needed for the family, which was no longer the chief institution for raising children to responsible adulthood. The rise of humanitarianism became a factor in promoting public education as a key to self-realization for the common man. Benjamin Franklin, Thomas Jefferson, John Locke, and Jean-Jacques Rousseau were all part of the background that emphasized the need for a school system.

Mann's campaign emphasized that adequate taxes for support of the common school were the cheapest means of self-protection and insurance. This was the message he spread when he was secretary of the House Committee on Education in Massachusetts. In 1874 the Michigan Supreme Court in the Kalamazoo Decision affirmed the right of the school board to levy taxes for public high schools.

Unfortunately, there are still issues to be resolved. Public education has done much to promote the well-being of its citizenry, but school systems still have a way to go. Maybe we can get it right by 2074. We had better hurry.

14

CAN AMERICAN STUDENTS COMPETE GLOBALLY?

National goals, such as educational goals, are based on national values. Japan, for example, has had a moral and ethical system based on three religions since the fifth century. Shinto, Confucianism, and Buddhism emphasize loyalty to authority and disciplined ways. These philosophies are sophisticated ethical systems.

America can be seen as a great contrast to the homogeneous Japan, in both people and values. Starting with Columbus in the fifteenth century, one finds a heterogeneous group of people from a number of different countries taking over the land from the Native Americans. These pioneering settlers and adventurers brought with them a fairly new conglomerate of cultures, attitudes, and morals.

In a perusal of books dealing with America's social heritage, especially David Hackett Fischer's *Albion's Seed*, it can be seen that the English, even though they were all from the same country, brought different sets of values to the areas of America where they settled. Their values were dependent on which part of England they had previously lived in. Those who had been living close to the borders of England settled in the Appalachians, and these English settlers had a fierce competitiveness, such as that seen in the biographies describing the youth of President Andrew Jackson, an Appalachian native.

Out of this multitudinous variety evolved the ideal of the individual. If a country as young as the United States can be considered to have a mythology, it can be seen in the "American tall tales." These stories, which emphasize independence of spirit and daring, are still taught to American elementary school children. The Paul Bunyan, Pecos Bill, and Davy Crockett stories are examples of this folklore found in children's schoolbooks. The admiration for the loner as a hero is seen in the Johnny Appleseed story. On his own he supposedly wandered all over the country sowing apple seeds. These folk heroes have many traits in common. They are adventurous. They go their own way, follow their own path, and are bigger than life in size and deeds.

There is a lot of bragging in these stories. These bigger-than-life adventurers seem to have the biggest mules, the ugliest dogs, the fastest axes, or whatever hyperbole fits their role. Many teachers have certainly listened to many children show this same level of oral bravado to their classmates, even though they had not done their homework or fulfilled classroom responsibilities. The similarities would be funny if they didn't bode so poorly for the student and the country.

No higher allegiance is seen in any of these tales, nor a sense of history, nor cooperative group interaction. Watching a few Charlie Chaplin films must have convinced the newly arrived immigrant from authority-heavy Europe that he had arrived in a country where there was a great deal of sympathy for the little man who defies authority—whether that authority is the neighborhood bruiser or the bank president. Indeed, he might have wondered if total anarchy was not the national idea.

History shows that around 1938 the National Education Association listed self-realization as the first goal of education. This was listed above human relations, economic competence, and civic responsibility. Academic excellence as a main goal was clearly not a primary direction for schools.

Many parents during the decades of the sixties, seventies, and eighties simply wanted their children to be happy in school. Homework that interfered with Little League baseball or organized football for ten-year-olds did not bring happiness to the family. It was not uncommon for teachers to receive notes from students' fathers and mothers, excusing their children from homework since the family needed to go visit someone or go shopping. If academic success is partially based on studying, one could deduce that good grades and high achievement in school were not paramount in the parents' minds. Fathers and mothers in parent–teacher conferences have often reiterated that they want a "good life" for their son or daughter, meaning a well-paying job. Sometimes parents want a better life for their son or daughter than they have, but academic success does not always seem the important key for them, as it does to the Japanese parent.

Our society's priority with regard to salaries may be partially responsible for the lack of interest in studying hard to get a good, high-paying job. In the nineties, a national newspaper for school children, *The Weekly Reader*, published an article showing the student readers the annual average salaries of different occupations. It pointed out the higher salaries of those in professional sports as compared to the lower salaries of teachers, the president of the United States, and other professionals.

In this same time period Japanese students had a longer school year than American students, and Japanese teachers received a salary that was 20 percent higher than the highest-paid civil servant job in Japan. It is obvious that these disparate attitudes are the basis for two very different cultures. Even when Japan was using some of America's educational techniques, the system was based on different cultural norms. It is fascinating to realize that in the 1920s the American philosopher and educational leader John Dewey was invited to Japan to explain his philosophy. Dewey's underlying philosophy was close to the Japanese idea of unity and development of cognitive, physical, and affective domains.

After World War II, the American occupation of Japan brought about changes in the outside structure of the Japanese educational system. Some of the implementations were a nine-year compulsory school period, rather than six years; development of comprehensive senior highs; part-time extension and correspondence courses; coeducational opportunities; junior colleges; general education in college curriculums; and teacher education in each national university (eliminating normal schools). The lower school curriculum implementation replaced Japan's morals classes with social studies.

The preamble to the United States' Education Mission to Japan document stated: "We shall esteem individual dignity and endeavor to bring up people who love truth and peace . . . education which is rich in individuality, shall be spread far and wide." This then brings us to the question of cultural values and the impact of principles on the importance of academic success. A society's culture influences, institutions, and schools can be seen as showing the strengths and weaknesses of certain values.

The efficiency of the Japanese education system rests upon the Confucian-based philosophy that includes perseverance as a virtue. Sustained effort is not an easy road, but if something comes easily in Japan, it does not confer value. One important result of a Japanese child's educational experience is the ability to commit intense effort to a task. Devotion to hard work itself is the mark of virtue. Nationally agreed-upon principles, such as perseverance, can be found in Japan's school syllabus: "It is desirable that, in the lower grades, one should learn to bear hardship, and in the middle grades, to persist to the end with patience and in the upper grades, to be steadfast and accomplish goals undaunted by obstacle or failure." There does not appear to be any such exhortation in the Los Angeles Unified School District, and I doubt if many public school districts in the United States have persistence and hard work as a goal.

Individual voices are trying to promote changes in our educational system. Nan Stone, as senior editor for the *Harvard Business Review*, put it plainly when she said, "In most United States public schools, students do not work hard. In 1988, more than two-thirds of United States high school seniors said they did one hour or less of homework each day." "If we seriously want American students to be better test takers, then we must demand that parents monitor two to three hours of homework each night and not allow their children to get cars and jobs. That is what the Japanese do!" said 1989 National Teacher of the Year Mary Bicouvaris.

Merry White in *The Japanese Educational Challenge: A Commitment to Children* addresses the eclecticism of American education. By emphasizing the value of the independent individual, we have difficulty establishing overall general guidelines to direct our system. This eclecticism shows up in the directives handed down to the classroom teacher. In the sixties teachers participated in training classes on set theory, the new "innovative" direction that math was taking, and many kindergarten students did learn quite a bit about sets and what sets meant at a primary level. After all the students were in that math program several years, and after many parent complaints, set theory went out of style. I recently heard that it might be coming back into vogue.

Just about every classroom teacher who has any length of time in the classroom will tell you that whatever is touted as new was probably already done twenty or thirty years ago. Phonics has been in and out, as have many other worthwhile techniques. As a nation, we are always looking for something better, and change sometimes seems better even if there are no criteria to show that it is. Therefore, one finds a diversity of approaches. There are free schools, fundamentalist religious academies, back-to-basics programs, open classrooms, elite prep institutions, and John Dewey–devised progressive schools. Students are being educated, but the academies and teachers involved do not participate in nationally established standards.

Fortunately, many teachers are delighted to remember how many students in their classes have shown miraculously high achievement at the same time that America is straining to find a consensus among parents, teachers, and policy makers that will permit a more systematic view of our own education system and the cultural conceptions that underlie it. We do have a cultural system of values based on the Founding Fathers' principles of independence, equality, and individualism, but the very independence of these values seems to have stymied America in finding common recognizable goals.

WHAT HAPPENS TO THE MENTALLY GIFTED STUDENT?

Many theories and opinions exist as to whether the academic needs of bright students need to be addressed separately, and if so, how. Some educators say that intelligent children succeed on their own, despite the system. Others want to promote special programs. Some demand that the bright boys and girls be integrated with all the students, and others promote separation.

It is probably difficult, at times, for the exceptionally bright student to fit into our society, a society that is dubious about the legitimacy of good grades and sometimes seems leery of intelligence. We still have films, cartoons, and books that make fun of the so-called nerds, turkeys, eggheads, four-eyes, or whatever demeaning term is presently being used.

Sometimes a very bright child will see many more possibilities in a teacher's direction than the other children perceive. Imagine one of those students. When his fourth-grade teacher tells the class to put their names and date on the paper, most just write their names anywhere. This student sees the task as an unclear problem that has to be solved. It is frustrating to him since he has a very high expectation of perfection for himself. The simple directive "put your name and date on the paper" is broken down by him as "left or right side, top or bottom, printed or cursive, should last name be first?" Even the date brings to mind alternatives. Does the teacher want just digits, or does the month have to be spelled out?

His need to satisfy his own personal level of perfection is excruciating to him. He has to do it correctly. His hand is constantly raised in order to check the directions given by the teacher. He spends most of the day, each day, with his hand up in the air questioning the exactness or the perceived ambiguities in the lessons that go on during class time. This student's fourth-grade teacher was tired out by his incessant need for exactness and did not want to teach the gifted clusters in fourth grade anymore after that year.

When the bright student came to a fifth-grade class the following year, that teacher tried to analyze how she could help him get along easier without feeling that there was so much ambiguity. It was the ambiguity that was paralyzing his ability to get on with the task. First, she tried to be very exacting in all directions that she gave. That meant that she started out the year by telling the class what to do verbally, and then she wrote it on the board, with examples, to clarify any mis-understanding.

Next, she spoke to the bright student privately and explained that sometimes it did seem as though there was more than one correct way to tackle a task. She told him that she wanted to make a deal with him. She would not hold him responsible for any mistakes. It was a promise from her. If he did the work differently than she had expected it to be done, or differently than the other students did it, it was all right. His grade would be just as good.

Old habits die slowly. Each time he raised his hand the week after her promise to him she shook her head gently and smiled reassurance. Soon he felt confident of the system she had arranged for him. He was a top student that year and no longer appeared to be as tense. This bright student went on in secondary school to garner national science awards. He did some very exciting scientific work. His teacher could see when he came back to visit his old fifth-grade classroom that he had a good sense of himself and what he could do with his intelligence.

A public school kindergarten teacher has all the five-year-olds. There did not seem to be separate programs for kindergarten children during the fifties and the sixties, although some five-year-olds needed special help or special classes. The structure of a good teacher's kindergarten class allows her or him to help each child at his or her own speed. However, as children mature, the learning gaps can become much larger as evidenced by the seeming "norm" in fifth grade of having students' reading level range from the second to the twelfth grade.

Even with five-year-olds, one can see what astonishment and dismay a precocious child felt when he first realized, upon contact with lots of other children, that what he knew and thought so naturally was not at all what the others thought or knew. Imagine a precocious boy who comes to kindergarten knowing all the correct terms for each era of dinosaurs and eager to discuss which classification came first and what kind of dinosaurs belonged to it. As he tried to talk and listen to his classmates, there appeared to be a look of confusion on his face. He realized that his classmates did not understand what he was talking about.

He started to isolate himself from the other children. He stopped talking to them and stood by himself. It was the teacher's job to help him understand what was happening, counsel his family, and hope he could find someone his age that had similar talents.

Being the outsider is never easy, no matter what the reason, and high intelligence can put one on the outsider path. Parents of bright children are often concerned about what kind of educational approach is best for their child. In the seventies, the Gifted Children's Association printed a story in their newsletter about an unusual approach to the problem of what to do with the precocious student in elementary school. Examples from that program follow.

The school's principal had developed a multigraded class for high-I.Q. students, and a teacher at that school had been asked to teach it. At the time, she had never considered leaving kindergarten. It was her great love, but then she realized that many of the students in this newly developed class were students she had taught when they were five-year-olds. That was too exciting a prospect to pass up.

The next September, she took over the MGM class of third through sixth graders. It was the state of California's program for bright children. To be designated as an MGM student, one had to be recommended by the teacher and tested by a school psychologist on an intelligence quotient test. Students who showed high I.Q. levels on the test were then qualified to receive academically enriched programs that were financially supported by the state.

The I.Q. level necessary to designate a child an MGM student seemed to change now and then. Sometimes the necessary cutoff was in the 130 range. Different designations were also made for highly gifted students, those getting scores of 140 or higher. At that time school psychologists were using the Stanford-Binet test. I.Q. testing had not yet become the political and social hot potato that it is today. Nevertheless, it was an issue that brought forth strong opinions. One father even demanded that the principal tell him the I.Q. of his child's teacher. This caused a small uproar throughout the school.

Many kindergarten teachers in the sixties had been trained to give the Pintner–Cunningham group I.Q. test to all the students in a class. Most teachers found it helpful as an additional tool to consider when evaluating a child's progress.

There were surprising advantages for the students in the MGM multigraded class. To begin with, it did not seem to matter if you were a third grader or a sixth grader. A brain that can function at a high level of critical thinking skills seems to be equally able to compete with those of older children in nonsocial activities. It was not immediately assumed that the older students would beat the younger students when they played chess or participated in logic games. The competition was based on skill in developing new strategies. It was good to see these bright students have equal competition. That way the winner did not feel that everyone thought he or she was the oddball who always won.

It actually seemed to give them a more relaxed attitude. I suspect this is because as humans we are always looking for a similar group to which we can belong. There had been a reasonable fear from the parents and teachers that this newly developed program would lead to a group of children who thought they were better than anyone else. Unfortunately, two years before the teacher in this example started teaching the class that seemed to have happened. The students in the class were considered to be rude. Teachers said that they felt the MGM group thought that they were privileged children who were above discipline and could get away with breaking the rules without any consequences.

I tend to think that intelligence quotients only indicate how we might perform academically. Thinking logically and participating in abstract work seem to be easier when one has a high I.Q. That means that intelligence is a tool that one can use if one decides to, but it is not to be used to make others feel inferior, or to feel superior about oneself. It is just something to make use of. Not everyone makes use of his or her intelligence. Teachers, parents, and researchers also know that emotional, social, or genetic factors are involved in how well a high I.Q. can be used.

The teacher of the MGM class could not control parents who wanted to feel superior and make others feel inferior, but she could and did explain her views to the students, and she let them know from lecture and experience that correct behavior was expected and was important. Happily, the students who had taken advantage of the previous situation caught on quickly and behaved themselves.

The staff and parents revised their opinion of the program. One teacher in first grade became so enthused about what the program could offer a smart child that she insisted that a very tall, bright first grader be placed in the third- to sixth-grade MGM class as a second grader, after he left her first-grade class. He was accepted as one of the group without hesitation.

The correctness of this class makeup was reinforced by what the students told her privately, as well as their academic progress. One girl had emigrated from Norway with her family. As the daughter of an artist she was immensely proud of her father's talent, but her first American school experience had not been satisfactory. Although she was very bright, she was also very shy. She was concerned about her accent and living in a new country. She had thought her previous isolated experience would be all that was available to her in her new country. Happily, she shone, as did all the others in the special multigraded class.

One young boy ended up in this class in third grade after he had been tested for mental retardation at his previous school. He was a below-average reader and hated school. His parents were from Mexico and family-life adjustments were difficult. He had hated school and had simply refused to put forth any effort. The school psychologist's tests showed that not only was he not below average in intelligence, he was above average. When he arrived at the school, he qualified for the MGM class.

It was, I expect, the stimulation of the similar thinking abilities of those around him that changed his life. Instead of staying at the second-grade level in reading comprehension, he zoomed by the year's end to the ninth-grade level, although he was still in the third grade. He also earned a starring role as king in the class play.

Fourteen years later, that teacher invited the students of the multi-graded MGM class to a reunion at her home. The boy in the previous paragraph had much to tell his former teacher about his memories of that special class. He explained that he had learned so much about himself. She was honored to listen to him speak of the importance he gave his elementary school years. He emphasized the significance of general knowledge that had been taught, as well as specific fond remembrances of chess, ceramics, square dancing, the Egyptian unit, papier-mâché, sign language, and preparing for the Renaissance Faire—which included costumes and language. He went on to say that many people might not think that the above studies make rocket scientists, but he felt that these are the things that shape young children into ambitious young adults.

Seeing so many children become mentally and socially comfortable and successful led many teachers to believe strongly in the program as it had been developed. There was laughter from one teacher when he realized that he could not or did not want to encourage the students to perform as the district's guidelines demanded. The MGM teacher for the school had to write up a proposal every year showing what the students would be doing that would be at a higher level of intellectual activity. It was also stipulated that the students must strive to achieve scores toward the ninety-eighth percentile on standardized tests. As the students were testing at the ninety-ninth percentile on these tests, one supposedly would have to ask them to study less, or think less. It was just one of those silly directives that make teachers wonder and laugh.

The cross section of ages in one classroom worked very well on several levels. The boys and girls had an ongoing community to belong to, and there was a sense of care and protection for each other. Children who had already been in the class, the older students, took on the role of explaining the independent work program and helping the younger ones develop their sports abilities.

Many teachers are not given any specific guidelines as to how one teaches four to five grade levels in one class, a class that is reminiscent of the old one-room red schoolhouse. But, this was one room within a school placed in a modern suburban setting. According to state guidelines, a differentiated curriculum, one that addressed higher cognitive functions, was to be the major direction of the class's work and study. This was a great challenge for the teacher and a continuing source of creative delight. One has to devise a new program every year for the four years that one might teach the class as most of the same students would be in the class the following September. The result is a different in-depth science unit for each school year, as well as a different unit for art, logic, and language. These units need to be much more extensive in their depth and breadth than the usual classroom work. Supplementary trips are paid for with state money. There is a certain dollar amount given each year per MGM student. If a large number of students in a school have been identified, the budget is larger also.

One year, the MGM teacher discovered that a class could attend the Renaissance Faire during the school week. These field trips were hard to get, as they were very popular. A coworker at the school with the special MGM program was so interested in what the children could do that she got a special date for the class through her brother, who had been an integral part of the Faire for years. The teacher was able to choose several study units for the class and signed them up for fifteenth-century games and Latin lessons. They received a list of fifteenth-century English terms that they were to use, as well as advice on what to wear. The Faire administrators were very strict about everyone staying in character for that century the whole day. All later discovered on the day of the trip, much to their annoyance, that no one on the premises would speak anything other than fifteenth-century English.

The children in the class were soon learning how to properly insult each other in the vernacular of that era, and several mothers came into the classroom with sewing machines. Within a few weeks everyone had a period costume. The teacher could arrange to get a school bus for the transportation there, but the bus could not pick them up as late as the Faire's program was scheduled. She did not want to cheat the students of one minute of what might be a once-in-a-lifetime experience. Fortunately the parents came through for the class. Car pools and cold lemonade in the late afternoon were provided for the thirsty and tired-out Faire participants.

Often, the special units, such as the one above, were developed in conjunction with what was going on in the city around them. During the year of the King Tut exhibit, the class studied the history of Egypt, visited the art show on Tut at the Los Angeles County Museum of Art, and made a six-foot by three-foot ceramic tile panel of Duamutef, one of the gods who surrounded the remains of Tut in the tomb.

Such a project might need help from the principal who could pick up the wood panel that is needed as a backdrop and bring it to the classroom. Then one student needs to volunteer to lie down on butcher paper so the class can trace a life-size human form. Next the boys and girls can sketch a life-size drawing of the god Duamutef, who watches over the stomach in the tomb. Finally, ceramic tiles need to be made and glazed. One is fortunate if the school has a working kiln. This large art piece, along with a fired and glazed chess set made up of Egyptian rulers on one side and symbolic gods on the other, can be taken to the area's local art show. Large shopping malls sometimes have annual art shows highlighting the creative endeavors of local school children.

Another year marine biology can be studied. The class can take trips on boats to watch whales, study the ocean temperature, and get a first-hand look at what is living at the bottom of San Pedro Harbor. A different year, birds might be the special science unit. After studying birds in general, each student can chose one that he or she wants to design and make in papier-mâché. It helps to have, as friends, two very talented former elementary school teachers to come to help with this project. One student might choose to make a peacock (using real feathers), one an ostrich, and one a hummingbird. The others might choose birds somewhat in between the sizes of the hummingbird and ostrich. These are to be life-size renditions.

Classes like these demonstrate that students need to express themselves well extemporaneously. The children have a lot of information inside their heads, but not enough experience in organizing it and presenting it orally. A good teacher can devise expert reports to help the boys and girls learn how to present their ideas, not only sequentially, but also in an interesting manner. The first year that one experiments with having the students present expert reports the twenty- to thirty-minute suggested presentation can go much longer. Imagine one student keeping the class, as well as the teacher, mesmerized for one hour on everything you might want to know about ants. It is exciting to realize how much the students can learn from each other. They may not have the graphics presentation that one gets from television, but they have the information and the enthusiasm.

Not everyone can give an outstanding presentation the first time around. Sometimes a student will only do enough work to present a report that earns him a "C" grade. His parents are aghast! They know he could do better. So does the teacher. The teacher's viewpoint has to be that he had the same chance as the others to study and perform. However, what he prepared was all that he had thought necessary, or all he had wanted to do. His folks still feel he could get a better grade if he did it over again. This is one of those times when the teacher has to be brave and think things through and stand alone. It is hard to say no. It is much easier to say yes, but good judgment tells one that the student had the same opportunity as everyone else, and he had to work hard enough the first time around for whatever it was he wanted. His parents will not be happy with that decision, and the teacher might very well feel uncomfortable with their uneasiness until the following year. Then, when that same student gives an outstanding report, an easy A, his parents tell the teacher how happy they are that she had helped their son realize the importance of doing a job well the first time around.

Parents can give mini–expert reports. It is important for the students to have some idea of what careers and job possibilities will be available to them later on in their lives. I also believe in parent participation. All parents can be invited to come to class to talk, anywhere from five minutes on, about their daily life at work. One can have parent presentations on different careers. The parent who is an English professor talks about writing poetry. A hairstylist teaches the students a lot about how hair grows, and a lawyer gets many questions from the class about what the day-to-day tasks of the profession are. Whatever the father or mother does for work is important, and they are to be welcomed with smiles, attentiveness, inquisitive questions, and hearty applause at the end.

It is rewarding and fun to see the parent's look of pleasure when they talk about their job in front of their child and their child's classmates. It isn't always easy for them, however. Sometimes a father, a professional musician, brings in his guitar and breaks into a heavy sweat with the strain of performing in front of his daughter's class. The parents will often tell the teacher at a later time how much they appreciated being included in their child's school day. One might even have to write a letter to the telephone company explaining that one of their employees was going to lecture on what is inside a telephone and how it works; otherwise that parent could not get the time off to participate.

Many of the MGM students are very good creative writers. In order to promote their interest in writing, one can put their prose and poetry into a small booklet. Part of their involvement can be a trip to the printer to understand the process a written piece of work goes through before it appears in a book. Each of the students receives a copy of the book showing their artwork and writing. Twenty years later, some of these authors will tell their teacher that they still remember what they and others wrote.

During the seventies, circle discussions were the "in" thing. The teacher would sit in a circle with a group of eight students (the others would have work to do at their desks). The group would focus on an emotional question for a period of about fifteen to twenty minutes. They needed to be far enough away from the working students that it was a rather private circle. No one had to talk or share, but everyone had the opportunity to talk without being interrupted or put down. The sense of security that had been established among their classmates led to some amazing openness.

The teacher usually started a group with the question "What was one of the most embarrassing things that ever happened to you?" After the teacher breaks the ice by explaining her chagrin at having her fifties-style starched petticoats stay on the ground around her feet after she stood up from a talk in the college quad with a male classmate whom she had wanted to impress, the circle members were eager to participate. The procedure was to just go around the circle so hands did not have to be raised. If someone passed the first time, the teacher would check after all the others had had their turns to see if the skipped person then wanted to talk. Usually everyone was eager to tell their story. What a treat to be able to talk without having people interrupt you with their own tale before you are through with yours.

After the embarrassing question, the teacher would go to more sensitive questions. When she posed the question "What is your greatest fear?" she was astounded to hear one student, in a quiet voice with tears in his eyes, relate that he was always afraid that his parents would die. The teacher had no idea that this was a prominent fear among elementary-age children until she saw the reactions of the group. Many felt the same way. There was no negative reaction to this sixth grader shedding tears as he talked about his fear. There was, instead, a genuine feeling of comradeship and understanding. I suspect it was a relief for this student to be able to talk about that fear. He was one of those students who did not seem to have any troubles in school and got along with everyone easily, one of those students whom people label just a happy-go-lucky kid.

The sense of community that this type of multigraded, ongoing class promotes is seen in the networking that occurs when these same students are in high school and need jobs. When one student calls his former teacher to fill her in on what is going on in his life, he mentions that he hasn't been able to find a part-time job. She has recently talked to one of his older classmates who is working at a fast-food place. After the teacher calls her, she telephones her former classmate, and he gets a job where she works.

How fortunate is the teacher who finds a career that has had so many lasting rewards, the rewards of watching the development of a whole group of young people as they come into their own.

IT DOESN'T COST ANY EXTRA MONEY

The experience of teaching the same children for more than one year shows that if the teacher likes the students, and the boys and girls get along with the instructor, it is a much more efficient program in terms of children learning more in a shorter period of time. Even teaching the same students two years in a row makes a difference in the speed with which one can get the boys and girls to get to work. Besides the above multigraded MGM class, one can have the opportunity to teach fifth graders one year who then stay on the next year as sixth graders.

Whether one's class was an MGM class, a high-achieving cluster class, an ESL cluster class, or a combination high-achiever and ESL class, they all had one commonality. These classes were predominantly multicultural, with many languages represented. The children love explaining about a native language other than English that is used in their family. This desire to share languages can be developed into a booklet with a dozen or more pages in it. Each page shows the lesson taught by a student volunteer from the class. The boys and girls should have the opportunity to teach the numbers one to ten as a start. The Chinese numbers usually so intrigue a class that they decide that they do not want to use those numbers for something as mundane as math. Sometimes, though, the students delight in the use of their booklets as they quiz each other on math problems. These booklets can be displayed on the students' desks on Open House evening and can help the parents to get an overall picture of the diversity in their child's class.

Teaching a little foreign language is one additional practice one can give the boys and girls speaking in front of a group. It is a fairly simple task, but often involves some adult help at home. Both parents and children seem to love this participation. It is surprising how many languages can appear during the time of presentations. Sometimes one can have Japanese, Korean, Chinese, Vietnamese, Farsi, Hungarian, Polish, Spanish, Russian, French, German, Tagalog, Hebrew, Italian, and different Indian dialects taught.

CLUSTERING

As the eighties arrived, the MGM program changed. It was now called the Gifted and Talented or GATE program. I suspect it was a statewide effort to try and include those students who might perform very well on achievement tests, but not on I.Q. tests. It also tried to address the student who is exceptional in areas other than academics. It was a large task, and the criteria used to determine if a student belonged in that category were not always clear. Many schools run a cluster program for GATE students. This is a commonly used grouping. Those students in one grade level who have been designated as GATE students are clustered within the makeup of one classroom.

This was the same period of time in Los Angeles when magnet schools had been designed to address the needs of exceptionally bright students. These were schools where everyone admitted would be an identified bright student according to the criteria of the times. Some of these institutions took just the bright; some took the very bright. These academies were developed to keep an ethnic balance in Los Angeles, in addition to other goals.

It was considered prestigious to be able to get into one of these public-run schools that often had waiting lists. One would think that all students would want to be in one of these schools, but that is not always the case.

Consider a student who had been enrolled in a fifth-grade class that became a fifth–sixth combination the next year. His family had already sent in an application to one of the highly gifted magnet schools. He was accepted the fall he started sixth grade, but decided to stay in the same room where he had already been the year before as a fifth grader. This was really a surprise to the teacher and showed the power of clustering and allowing a teacher to teach the same students more than one year.

16

WHAT HAPPENED TO THE BILINGUAL STUDENT IN THE EIGHTIES?

In the seventies, schools were trying to address the educational needs of immigrant students. Suddenly there seemed to be many students who were not speaking English, or not very much English. Some students spoke Vietnamese, others Armenian, and a growing number spoke Spanish. The percentage of these students had grown to such a large number that the district guidelines, based on the California LAU case concerning the responsibility of a school system to provide English language instruction, mandated a special program for them. This involved extra money and new directives. Schools were trying to fill in the gaps and attend to the needs of these students.

New rules demanded that the boys and girls have primary-language instruction available to them. It was to be taught by their teacher, and if a properly credentialed teacher with the needed language proficiency could not be found, funds were available to hire a bilingual aide. There were also funds to acquire texts in the primary language of the student. The available texts tended to be in the Spanish language, not Vietnamese, or Japanese, if one could find any that had been published.

This state-mandated program resulted in an administrative overload. Teachers, at the same time that they were teaching, were trying to administer the funds and deal with the administration of the program. That was not realistic. Some faculties saw the need for a full-time bilingual coordinator to oversee the program for the school. In some cases, there was enough money to pay a teacher to be out of the classroom eight hours a day in order to administer and enforce the bilingual guidelines, and there was certainly enough work to keep one busy every moment. Sometimes this position was made available to everyone on the faculty. Teachers who were interested in applying for the job had often completed a master's degree and had an administrative credential.

At that time, bilingual education directives allowed parents to choose between two types of programs for their kindergarten child. If the child was not already reading in his or her native language, the Spanish-speaking parent could choose to have the child in a bilingual program where he or she would receive instruction in Spanish and English. Proficiency tests in Spanish and English would have to be passed before the child could enter an English-only program. The alternative was to place the child in an ESL class. These children would have an aide—hopefully one was available—who knew their language. They would receive extra help in acquiring English and only have to pass proficiency tests in English.

The bilingual coordinator might have a bilingual aide who could come into the school office to explain the program options to the parents of new kindergarten children before they were enrolled. Many parents, at that time, chose the ESL approach. Students whose native languages were other than English or Spanish were in that program also, as the personnel for all needed languages were not available. In the sixties, many people marched for civil rights and raised voices against discrimination. But in Los Angeles in the seventies, if your native language was not a language spoken by a certain number of other students, there would not be a bilingual program for it.

Students in a bilingual program had to pass proficiency tests in two languages. I saw this hamper some students. Students who took longer to master academic material, or who were not what is termed "test wise," were kept from progressing to the next step in the program. The rules governing the bilingual program seemed to be discriminating against the Spanish speakers in Los Angeles as those were most of the students who had to pass tests in two languages, when others, including the ESL students, only had to pass one test.

The obvious preference by district administration for a bilingual rather than ESL approach was evident when one school was monitored and rated by a team as to how well they were implementing the program. Although they had followed the guidelines exactly as written in explaining the two alternative programs in kindergarten to parents whose children spoke a language other than English, the examining team was upset because more parents had chosen the ESL program than the bilingual option. That was their choice. However, the rating team indicated they should have prompted these parents to choose the bilingual-only approach.

It was also a time when a good teacher realized how effective one could be if one was not prejudiced. Parents and children seemed to sense that color, ethnicity, or nationality were of no consequence to some teachers. This allowed them the freedom to be honest and helpful.

Three years of administering that type of program taught some teachers that, as far as they were concerned, the real excitement and action in education is in the classroom. A teacher who left that position, stayed at the same school, and resumed teaching in a bilingual fifth-grade class would be shocked at what the reality of the bilingual program was for some children.

Teaching those bilingual children showed that teacher where the program had not sufficiently helped the students. Vocabulary development had not been rich enough in many cases to allow the boys and girls to be properly tested on a concept. Students could be taught how to outline, but a proper testing device requires a different vocabulary than that used to teach the concept. So, as an example, when an outline needed the words *sofa*, *chair*, and *table* to be categorized under the heading of "furniture," the children who were not familiar with the term *furniture* would not be able to show their basic proficiency in the concept of outlining. It was very frustrating. Bilingual teachers taught a lot of vocabulary. They were always explaining words, more than they had ever needed to before. It was tiring, but necessary.

It was obvious that many of the boys and girls in that class were quite bright, and they were eager to learn. Their teacher felt that in math they would have the greatest opportunity to show their ability. Less reading and more thinking was required in arithmetic, and so each morning the class would review five problems on the board, in addition to their regular math instruction period.

That particular year, the district was changing the makeup of elementary schools and junior highs. Elementary schools were to change from a kindergarten through sixth grade to kindergarten through fifth. The junior highs were now called middle schools, and these newly defined institutions changed their enrollment by picking up the sixth graders while sending their ninth graders on to high school. Due to this change, the junior high teachers were anxious to analyze the math levels of the new sixth graders they would get in September. A math assessment tool was devised by them and sent to the fifth-grade teachers. Since this was a newly developed test, no teachers or students had previously had the opportunity to know what was on it. This made it a more legitimate test as one could not study for it ahead of time.

The bilingual teacher's belief in the native intelligence of her class, along with the extra daily drill, paid off. After all the fifth graders at her school had taken the test, a listing of students' names and scores from the three fifth-grade classes was sent from the junior high to my school. Besides the three fifth-grade classrooms, there was a group of thirteen gifted fifth graders from a GATE cluster. Out of the top seventeen scorers, eleven of them were from the bilingual group. This certainly beat the odds!

There were other lessons to be learned from that group. When that teacher would walk her class out for physical education, the students seemed to take over the asphalt as they walked in front of her to the baseball diamond. She heard that other teachers referred to her class as the "beef trust." Although the boys in her class that year seemed to outweigh the other fifth graders and appeared tough and streetwise in their demeanor, they were courteous and hard workers. The bilingual teacher didn't know whether it was a coincidence or not, but her room was not vandalized when many others were repeatedly broken into that year. She suspected that the sense of pride that the students had in their classroom had permeated the community, and no one was going to mess with them.

It is hard for a shy child who is bilingual to become comfortable conversing in a class. Good teachers have always expected students to participate in group discussions and to answer teacher-directed questions. Imagine a child who defied that expectation. She absolutely refused to answer any question submitted to her, even though her teacher felt sure that she understood the question. She would sit mute and defiant. When the teacher asked why, the other girls in the class explained to her that the girl had never, ever, opened her mouth in the fourth-grade class. A little investigation was needed. The girl had come to the school in the middle of fourth grade and was placed into a classroom with a teacher who was considered to be somewhat abrasive and caustic to students.

With that knowledge, her teacher figured that the girl had just been protecting herself. It was necessary for the teacher to keep her after class and explain to her that she needed her to answer. The teacher needed it a lot. The girl was told that she would never be embarrassed in front of her classmates. The two set up a program where the teacher would ask her a simple question, ending with, "Do you agree?" Her task was to nod and say yes. They practiced a couple of times.

The next day, the teacher caught the girl's eye ahead of time, smiled, and asked a question in the form they had set up. That teacher was holding her breath, willing a simple yes as hard as she could. The girl did respond. Whew! The teacher stayed with that regimen for several weeks. As the girl became more relaxed, the teacher could add more complexity to the questions directed to her. Success! But sometimes success can backfire on the teacher. By the end of the year, that student, during class time as well as after school, was asking so many questions that it was exhausting the teacher. The girl was smart, and she did make her teacher work for her.

It was a period of time when the Spanish-speaking children in the school had usually migrated from Mexico or El Salvador. Some came into the class midyear. One such student appeared to be a quiet Salvadoran who spoke only Spanish. The teacher immediately introduced her to his bilingual aide and had the aide give her and two others, at a similar academic and language level, special attention daily.

Several days after the new girl had been in the class, the other girls quietly pointed out to the teacher that this new student only had one arm. She was exceptionally adept at standing or sitting so one only saw clearly her left side, where she had an arm. It was explained to the teacher that she had been too close to a machine in a milling plant, and the arm was severed near the shoulder. That child had a good year in the class, and when she left for middle school, she had a prosthetic arm to go with her. The school nurse and her teacher had worked together to get the proper agencies to help. Small miracles can keep happening.

17

THE CLASSROOM TEACHER'S IMAGE ON TELEVISION

Looking at the public image of the American school teacher in television programs, one can see a chronological portrayal that reflects the changes in our society since the fifties. At first, television characterized teachers as dolts and incompetents. Miss Brooks of the *Our Miss Brooks* series, which ran from 1952 to 1956, is shown as a slightly wacky teacher. She was the classic example of a negative stereotype—the female teacher who was unmarried and sexually frustrated. Situations abounded in this television comedy in which the teacher was the butt of ridiculous male–female jokes. Her coworkers did not fare any better. They were depicted as buffoons. This was a series that degraded the teacher as a person and teaching as a profession. One change that started during this time era was that male teachers, rather than female teachers, were portrayed in popular television series.

The *Mr. Peepers* series, which ran from 1952 to 1955, showed the teacher as a nonheroic, uninvolved, comic individual. Mr. Peepers, while well intentioned, was an inept bumbler in his personal life. He was seen as a childlike man who had great knowledge about an esoteric area of biology. However, the humdrum day-to-day problems of life were too much for him. He could not cope. Basically, he was the little mild-mannered man peering out at the world from behind overlarge spectacles.

Interestingly, the *Mr. Novak* series, produced from 1963 to 1965, brought new dimensions of the teacher to the screen. For the first time on television the teacher was seen as a hero figure. He was a tall, attractive man who would stride through the halls with a sense of purpose. He knew he was a good teacher, and he knew that teaching was important. Mr. Novak was a soldier who had decided during the Korean War that what counted in this world was education. He then set out to be a teacher, a good, conscientious, intelligent professional. He was mainly concerned with the academic side of his job: were the students learning what they needed for their future lives? He taught at a college-oriented high school where the majority of the students went on to higher education.

This series could have been used as a basis for a high school English class's curriculum. While grammar was being taught, Novak would say, "I know you find this dull. You've had it in ninth grade, in tenth grade, but maybe this is the year it's going to get easy." In addition to studying grammar, his students were asked to analyze plays and poems. Novak was the ideal in terms of the traditional, subject-oriented teacher. To him learning could be challenging, exciting, or hell. It all depended upon the teacher. As a teacher, Novak was concerned about his students' social and psychological well-being, but his main job was to teach and to teach well. The program presented a theme of urgency about teaching—"life is precious: information, knowledge and wisdom, not bullets, can solve the problems of this world."

Should exceptions be made for students who do not fulfill academic standards if they are exceptionally talented athletically? The *Novak* series presented this problem as the plot theme in one program. When pressure was brought by the principal, fellow teachers, and the boy's family to be lenient and pass the student regardless of his English grades, Novak stood by his principles. The student did not get to pitch for the visiting scouts.

The television image of the schoolteacher since the 1960s has often been that of a strong, intelligent, attractive, and caring professional. Television has also shown teachers growing toward the role of social psychologist. In *Lucas Tanner*, a 1974–1975 series, it was emphasized that the teacher was more of a counselor than an academician. He was more concerned with his students' problems than with their mastery of curriculum. Tanner's devotion to academic responsibilities was less strong than his desire to lend a helping hand to those in need. When a fellow coworker was absent due to emotional problems, Tanner called for a substitute for his own class in order to counsel the faculty member at her home. It was this portrayal of the teacher that made the series so popular. Just as everyone wants a doctor like Marcus Welby (as seen in a 1970s TV program), one who has infinite patience, interest, and time to invest in every patient, so would everyone like to have such a teacher.

The *Welcome Back, Kotter* series of 1975–1979 presented a teacher who was dramatic and flamboyant in his methods. He could be classified as a nontraditional teacher, one whose role had evolved to that of a psychologist and social worker. The viewer saw a classroom group of about twelve students who spoke out, wisecracked, and generally misbehaved in the school setting. These students had been labeled as nonlearners or slow learners. They were troublemakers, and Kotter was trying to keep them entertained. A lot of Kotter's time was spent counseling his students at his home. Students appeared at his apartment at odd hours, climbing through the window to ask for his help and advice with their social problems. He was seen as a surrogate father figure.

The next important series was a program with a dramatic name. One would not necessarily realize that *The White Shadow* was the title of a series about a high school teacher. Ken Reeves, known as the White Shadow, was a coach whose main job, besides teaching basketball skills and winning games, seemed to be to straighten out his students psychologically. In this series, there were episodes where the setting was not even the school. An example was the program where Ken had his students help him move to his new apartment. The theme revolved around the theft of a bottle of wine and the alcoholism of one of his students.

Education in the socially changing decades of the sixties and the seventies felt the influence of psychologists William Glasser, Abraham Maslow, and Carl Rogers. The result was an educational system that became more socially oriented and less academically oriented. An observable concurrent direction could be seen in the television programs. Novak emphasized the importance of studying to students. His advice to them was "Dropouts are the bottom of the barrel! What kind of a job can you get without a high school diploma? What kind?" The trend away from traditional teaching started with Tanner, who spent a lot of his time dealing with his students' nonacademic problems. He wanted to be an advisor because of his interest in the "whole" child. Where a curriculum guide for English could be developed from the Novak series, case studies could be compiled from the Tanner series.

Social engineering was seen even more strongly in Kotter's classroom techniques. This class was portrayed as being so unruly that one voice at an assemblage of TV editors and critics was heard to say, "I don't like those kids at all, and if I were a teacher I wouldn't go near them!" The series was banned in Boston. Unfortunately, too often this seems to be the public's view of schools. The discipline in *The White Shadow* was so poor that at one point we see the teacher socking a student after being attacked by him.

Over the years, even the titles of the series show a changing image of the teacher. The *our* in *Our Miss Brooks* sounds proprietary, as though she belongs to the public, not herself. *Mr. Peepers* implies a shy, ineffectual sort of man. *Mr. Novak* is a traditional title. *Lucas Tanner* is less formal. The *Mr.* is dropped, and the first name is added. *Welcome Back, Kotter* uses the teacher's last name only—a casual approach—and *The White Shadow* uses a nickname that conjures up high adventure rather than classroom routine.

I realize that when I started teaching in the fifties, I felt some of the stigma attached to the profession. There was an awareness of society's implied allegation that if you were really smart you would be doing something else, something that had more prestige and paid a better salary. I remember telling people at a cocktail party that I was a landscape artist when the casual conversation turned to jobs. I was curious to see if there would be more interest evidenced than if I had told them I was a kindergarten teacher. I was too new at the job at that time to realize how many people, students and parents, would feel that what I did made a difference in their lives. That was the joy of fulfillment and awareness that came years after being in the classroom day after day, year after year.

Now, I am and have been thrilled to tell people that I dedicated thirty-eight years of my life to the teaching profession. Teachers and police officers are at the cutting edge of what is going on in our society. It is an exciting and challenging opportunity to participate in a worthwhile activity.

PART 4

This section provides examples of techniques and values that promote the success and good behavior of students. It is meant to be a guide for parents, teachers, and concerned citizens who wish to have the best possible educational system for their young people.

I have witnessed too many talented people drop out of the teaching field because no one taught them the strategies of classroom management or control. By *control* or *management*, I mean a classroom atmosphere where, generally speaking, everyone is focused on the learning task, being responsible for himself or herself, and having a good time as well, for learning is a stimulating high. Even more disturbing than the rate of teachers dropping out is the large number of new teachers who are hurried through a teacher-training program or intern program and are "hanging in there" but whose classrooms are disruptive, disturbing environments.

Many teachers need more training. They need the ability to discipline through the use of logical and natural consequences. Discipline is generally considered the number one problem facing American schools today. One hears over and over that teachers in general lack the training and resources for effective classroom management. Here are tried and true techniques that work in today's classroom. I'm talking about a classroom in Los Angeles, the second largest urban city school system in our country!

18

BELONGING AS A GOAL

The most important concept that I have discovered is the strong need today's student has for a sense of community. Students, whether from well-to-do professional families or from poor, uneducated families, are quite isolated. Parents, if there are two, are often stressed and over-worked, with little time for parenting. Our society no longer has much in the way of extended families or church communities. To fill this void I have learned to create what I think of as a tribal feeling in my class-room. Students thrive when they find solidarity with their fellow class-mates. There needs to be a sense of community, security, and challenge in the classroom today.

An unusual sense of belonging can be consciously developed in the classroom. As a result, when something good happens to one of the stu-dents, there is usually a spontaneous outburst of applause, claps on the shoulder on the way to recess, and many congratulatory remarks from the other students. There should be a sense of pride that all feel from the achievement of anyone in the class. This acts as a natural motivation.

I have always advised student teachers to develop a good classroom climate that is warm, supportive, and pleasant. Students perform better in a climate of security and mutual trust. Subject matter needs to be taught at an appropriate level with an emphasis on good timing.

Room 5 specialness. (That was my classroom number. The number is, of course, the number of your own room.) I would say to the class, "You are special because you are here in this room. I don't understand it, but for the last three years since I have been at this school, everyone has said the students in Room 5 are the best." Children love a sense of mystery and a feeling of belonging. It is best to always refer to the class members as students, not children or boys and girls. You can say, "Look, you are already proving the point, I can see that you are exceptional." As visitors come into the class on errands, especially if they are adults, you can say, "Did you ever see such a great group?" You should be very enthusiastic and smile a lot as you say this. Being an amateur ham is a real asset.

All of this positive reinforcement leads to a group or tribal feeling. Pride in their classmates and pride in what can be done if they all scheme and plan together promotes such a feeling of well-being, even joy. Here is an example. Prizes can be given by the school for the best class at the lunch table. During lunch, teachers are duty free, so you are not around your class physically. Explain to the class that if they want to win the prize, it will be a little bit like the "game of life" and teach them how to play. The problem can be presented to the class as follows: "How are the noon-duty aides going to see our room is quiet when all they hear is noise from eight other rooms? Aha! We will pretend we're in a play and act. Here is our acting part. When the aides blow the whistle [a signal for quiet], everyone, without laughing, sit tall and straight, clamp lips shut and fold hands on tables. If everyone does it [group cohesiveness], the aides will be so amazed that they'll pay attention."

The teacher must remind the students before they go out to lunch, "Remember our play—remember to act—don't laugh!" It helps to smile at them, reassuring them that you are on their side. After lunch, run up excitedly. "Did it work? What happened?" You should give everyone time in class to talk about it. Actually, you are establishing class cohesiveness. They will win the prize. The noon-duty aides might even come in the room to commend and exclaim about their behavior. An additional outcome is the feeling that the students now trust your judgment. You can be trusted to lead them. It is of the utmost importance that students understand that the teacher is fair, trustworthy, and in charge.

This type of group feeling may show up later when a student doesn't have a lunch. Immediately, a number of students will offer money or extra food from their lunches. A good feeling about caring for one another has been established.

STRATEGIES

The essentials are the smile and eye contact. Make sure that the smile is genuine. Children are quick to pick up on any phoniness and insincerity. A smiling face is reassuring to children and helps them feel that you are on their side, an ever-important point to them. Eye contact is a remarkably effective tool. When they see that you are keeping an eye on them and care about their behavior, they seem to sense that this is indeed a matter of importance. Also, none of us seems to want to be seen doing that which we ought not to be doing. Know what you are teaching that day and have all materials prepared and ready. You cannot smile and have eye contact while you are checking page numbers or correcting yesterday's papers.

RULES

Let the rules be known right away. If you are a new teacher, preface the rules with "You don't know what's important to me yet, so I'd like to let you know." If you've been at the school several years, you can preface by saying, "You've probably heard what is really important to me." Then elucidate. I'd say the following: "I will not get angry at you if you get a bad grade or get mad at someone and get into a fight. I will get very angry if, when I ask you to stop doing something, you ignore me, and if you purposely hurt other people's feelings."

It is up to you, as the teacher, to decide what is of the utmost importance to you. We can't do everything, but we surely can do some things exceptionally well if we've internalized what it is that we want.

EXPECTATIONS

Spell out your expectations that first day or two. Say something like, "I expect you to listen to me when I'm talking. I get paid to talk, and I have important things to tell you. I promise not to talk so much two weeks from now. You watch, I'll keep that promise. I will not talk or interrupt you while you are talking. I will not allow anyone else to, either." "I do not make fun of people whose ideas are different than mine, and I will not allow others to make fun of students in this class." "These are things I'm very strict about. In other areas, there are a lot of freedoms in our room."

CONNECTING WITH THE STUDENT

When you find yourself angry at a student and want his or her behavior changed, talk quietly to the student.

1. Make eye contact. If the student is seated at a desk, go to the desk, lean over, and smile as you make the request.
2. Make the request seem like something you and the student are conspiring to do together: We can do it—I'll help you.
3. Take the student into the hallway where other students cannot clearly see you. That way, other students are not watching to see the troubled student's reactions. This releases the student's defenses.
4. Students often want to do what you ask, they just need help—concrete means and ideas.

FUN

A wonderful strategy is the basic premise that school should be fun—learning should be fun. We may all have the same curriculum or texts to use in our classrooms, but the creative teacher finds a way to make the lesson interesting, even fun. What a challenge. As a teacher you won't find yourself bored if you're always searching for an even better, more interesting, more efficient way to present the concept.

First, survey a new class to know their needs as a group. It is good to always check with the previous year's teachers for an overview. Do the students need a lot of security and structure? Are they self-motivated? Are they whizzes academically? How do they relate to each other? An example: if you hear that your new class of fifth graders will be slow, unmotivated, and unable to handle excitement, you must consider how to organize for their needs.

The first or second day of class, borrow the fourth-grade math books from the teacher across the hall. Then, ask the class to show you what they remember from last year by solving the thirty-three problems on the last page of the fourth-grade math book. It is usually an end-of-the-book test page. Explain that test courtesy requires quiet if they finish early. Free-time reading books should have been placed at each desk in case they finish early. This is a technique that can be used for all tests, as a good teacher doesn't believe in wasting time. Time and ease (efficiency of your use of time) means that you should have the students work the problems first on scratch paper. They then transfer the answers to a lined piece of paper that you have cut (a half sheet of 8½ × 11). It is easier if they all follow the same numbering system (1–20 on the front of the sheet and 21–33 on the back).

You might be aghast to see that the students, students from three separate classrooms, all fail. What to do? The answer seems to be three math lessons a day. The first lesson is on the new concepts to be taught at the fifth-grade level (a short seven-step lesson). Then you can develop a fun math lesson as a break. Show them that math can be as much fun as a game.

During this break time you can teach them how to play a game where one has a certain number of toothpicks in a geometric pattern and when one moves a certain number, one has a new pattern. This is a thinking lesson, not a paper and pencil lesson, and it works well when played by two students helping each other. Visual perception tasks can also be used at this time, such as a game where the goal is to copy a figure without crossing a line.

It is also great if you can teach them how to play chess. (Have enough sets for everyone in the class to play.) Today's students have little opportunity to develop cooperative learning patterns at home. Most go home to an empty house, or babysit a younger sibling. With working parents, it may not be safe for them to have friends over or to go to someone's home where there is no adult supervision. Teaching chess serves several purposes. First, your rainy-day recesses and lunches are taken care of, high-level thinking patterns are used, strategy is a natural, and the final result is learning to play a game and get along with each other.

After the fun math break, there needs to be a short review lesson of concepts they need to know and have forgotten. Perplexed students might query, "Are you a math expert?" "No," you can reply, "not until this class." Don't forget to smile. This format can be used in any subject area that is particularly weak and needs extra attention.

After the first test, you can develop two groups that have the possibility of a change of membership after every new math test. Call one the Math Club and the other the Review Club. One of the bulletin boards can have a caption that reads "Math Club." After every new math test, the new 90 percent and above tests are pinned up on that board. Old tests go home. At this time a new schedule might evolve. Everyone receives instruction at the same time on the new concept. It makes a lot of sense to students to write the concept they're learning at the top of their work-page before they begin to work. It is important for them to hear, see, and write what it is they are learning. Some days there can still be a math break of fun math. After that, the Math Club moves to desks at one side of the room for a choice of activities. Some choices (they should change from month to month) can be folding really fancy hard-to-make paper airplanes (*More Best Paper Aircraft* by Campbell Morris, 1988, is a great book), origami, painting, free drawing with new felt pens (only used at that time), playing chess, and extra time on the computer with games like King's Rule, an advanced number pattern game. An extra bonus is the opportunity to demonstrate to the entire class how their planes fly. The paper airplane flights then culminate the day's math lesson.

At the same time, the Review Club students are at their seats. They work with you slowly and tutorially on one review problem at a time. An innovation after the third math test is to allow the B or C students the opportunity to help F or D students. Note: No one is really an F, D, C, B, or A student; these letters simply represent test scores on one particular test—there is always the possibility for a change at the next test. You must make up the pairings—thinking carefully about individual personalities, and, of course, no one is referred to as a B or D student. They are tutors and tutees. Tutors should be taken outside into the hall for an explanation of the program. The concepts of patience and correct procedure must be stressed.

Explain the incentive as follows: "Gee whiz, I'm so sorry you missed the Math Club by just 10 lousy points. I tell you what! If your tutee passes the next test with at least 70 percent, you will get ten extra-credit points on your score on the next test. So, if on the next test, in three to four weeks, your tutee gets 70 percent or better, your ten extra-credit points added onto 80 percent would be 90 percent, or if you had 95 percent, you'd get 105 percent. You can't lose. You have to study and review anyway. By teaching someone else you learn better yourself. There is no penalty if your tutee doesn't pass. Can't lose! Go to it!"

You will be amazed at the success of this program. It works! The innate joy of learning, helping, and succeeding infuses everyone with a glow! On the first try, two student pairings out of eight might be a success from the standpoint of passing and getting extra credit. Suddenly Review Club students are anxious to have tutees to help.

Additionally, a new close friendship may develop between a Chinese-speaking girl and a Spanish-speaking girl. The Spanish-speaking student may be the tutor, not the tutee. An adult visitor to the class may erroneously assume the Chinese girl is the tutor. One can see this as a classic case of stereotyping, which this program helps dispel. In another case, two boys, one a very popular athlete and one a new bused-in student from a different area, may become friends and grow to appreciate each other and their ethnic differences.

You will be pleased to hear from students, as well as parents, that school is exciting and math is fun for the first time. Standardized test results at the end of the year can be expected to show an increased stanine point average for the class. In some cases, an improvement of four points can be made for an individual student.

BASIC VALUES

For a number of years now, I have been aware that there are some basic values, which, when adhered to, seem universal enough to cover all instances of misbehavior and racial or ethnic grouping or slurs. I developed these after teaching thirty-four years in the Los Angeles Unified School District and taking many multicultural and ethnic diversity education classes. Equality demands the following:

- Responsibility
- Respect
- Consideration
- Sensitivity

Using these four values as my rule of thumb, I have not had insolvable problems of discrimination or the ganging up on one group by another group.

It is hard to separate the four values above. By respecting the students and demanding respect from them for you, and for and from each other, you can develop a group of students who evidence a responsible attitude. This also relates to being considerate of one's classmates and teacher. This type of sensitivity should be expected. The students should expect to receive responsibility, respect, consideration, and sensitivity from you. This sets the standard for them to give and expect to receive these same values from each other.

Respect can be shown by you toward students in many ways. Students accept this respect by engaging in responsible behavior. Simple examples are bathroom privileges and pencil sharpening privileges. Explain to a class that, at their age (ten to twelve), you do not see any reason why they should have to ask permission to use the bathroom. School safety regulations require that you always know where everyone is, so an effective technique can be the bathroom box. This is a 5" × 5" square drawn on the lower corner of the chalkboard. Students wishing to use the bathroom put their initials in the box and leave the room quietly. On their return, they erase their initials.

It is the student's responsibility to not abuse the privilege and to show you respect by not leaving while you are involved in a directed lesson. This is the same respect shown if a class member is talking, reciting a poem, or leading a class discussion. Visitors or guest lecturers receive the same respect. Here then is an obvious overlap between responsibility, respect, sensitivity, and consideration. I have noted that there are usually two or three students a year who need help by my admonishing them quietly and privately not to abuse the privilege. Privileges given by one's teacher are, of course, quite easily taken away for a certain period of time.

Pencil sharpening is a must. One luxury a teacher can indulge in is buying an electric sharpener for the classroom. Students, one at a time (no lines may form), are welcome to sharpen their pencils whenever a lesson is not being taught. You should not have to wait before a lesson or test for pencils to be sharpened. Be adamant. Give out crayons or old pencils if they have to have a writing implement. Pencils should be sharpened during the afternoon, when there is a good hour of silent reading.

This shows respect and consideration for the value of the students' time, since they don't have to wait around, doing nothing, while someone sharpens a pencil. It is also another way to teach and reinforce responsibility.

Strategies to curtail busy, mundane work to a small and efficient time span are important in keeping the students interested and eager to participate in the next activity. Eager, interested students are usually attentive and ready to go, as they haven't been bored to death by waiting around. Waiting around is the most difficult time for students. It is hard to be on task when the only task is waiting for things to be explained or materials to be passed out.

Chores, such as passing out papers or books, can be handled with a minimum of fuss and disturbance by using monitors. Designate a student paper monitor and a student book monitor for each row. That is their responsibility. When you are ready to disseminate materials, ask for monitors. They receive the materials from you or pick them up from a shelf. They do the necessary counting and passing out of materials themselves. Everyone in the room should have a job. Everyone. Everyone deserves enough respect to be responsible for a job. This increases the feeling of responsibility to the class (their community). It develops a sense of interdependence and increases their sense of self-esteem and respect. It is, incredibly, the feeling of being valuable—I am a valuable person—that is essential to mental health and is a cornerstone of self-discipline. Classroom jobs develop that sense of being important.

One of the teacher's roles is to develop the students' self-esteem. It is the teacher's consideration, sensitivity, and respect for the student that results in planning that helps the student find himself/herself in an atmosphere that leads to greater self-esteem. Jobs in a classroom should last for a semester (five months), half the school year, and then be rotated. The president is elected, as are team captains. Elections can be held about the second or third week of a new school year. Explain that it would be inconsiderate to pupils new to the school to hold elections earlier. It is important to show evidence of the validity of values in day-to-day experiences.

It is also important to be sensitive to the feelings of the nominees for office. The election can be an exercise in correct democratic procedure, but you must be careful about how it is run. Small pieces of paper, to be used as a ballot, are handed out by you. Voting takes place by choosing one candidate from the several nominations on the board. That name is quickly, quietly, and secretly written on the paper. The paper is then folded in half. Circle the room to pick up the ballots. You should tally the results in the teachers' lunchroom and report the outcome to the class after lunch.

The runners-up are then told that they are the classroom team captains. If there are more than three nominations, tell the others that you have written down their names and will call upon them to work as alternate team captains when the president is absent.

Team captains have very prestigious jobs. They garner a lot of respect from the responsibility given them. During physical education sessions they select the two teams. This is done out of eyesight and earshot of the rest of the class. The captains' task is directed by you. They are to select an even number of girls and boys and best, medium, and worst players for each team. They are never to tell anyone who was chosen first or last. This helps the captains understand the importance their teacher gives to consideration and sensitivity. They develop these values as they assume their duties. They choose carefully who will be up first, letting an even number of boys and girls have that chance. The captains have the option to discuss and make changes in the teams. This is usually done if the teams are lopsided in most competitions. They also have the responsibility of choosing a game to play on Fridays, of keeping score, and of solving any disputes that arise during a heated game.

The students (players) are not to come to you with their complaints. They can talk to their team captain, who may then consult with you out of ear range of the teams. The captains may also consult with each other and come to a decision. These consultations take place a distance from the teams so no one is yelling advice to them or pressuring them. There is usually never a reason to challenge any of their decisions or bad feelings after very competitive games. Students are being respected by not being in a position where someone can make fun of them. It is interesting to note that the fifth-grade class president and team captains often go on the next year to more elevated positions of school leadership as student council officers.

Traffic patterns are also easy ways to keep even sixth-grade classes well ordered and efficient in their use of time. It is easy to review geography at that time. One might tell one row to line up at the north door or to pass their papers to the west for collection. When everyone moves simultaneously, it tends to seem chaotic. Less movement at one time allows you to see that everything is proceeding smoothly. Those who might not yet be as considerate as one would wish have less chance to demonstrate or get into the habit pattern of inconsiderateness.

(22)

CAUSE AND EFFECT

Discipline and order do not necessarily mean punishment. Discipline can be based on responsibility, respect, consideration, and sensitivity. Students do need to know who is in charge, however, and there should be no doubt in their minds that it is you. They need to have a teacher who is willing to take the responsibility of being in charge.

A cause and effect system can be used efficiently when students are still practicing the above values and haven't yet completely succeeded. If you hurt someone or annoy him or her by throwing acorns or eucalyptus pods (many of which fell to the ground daily from our abundant trees), it does not seem unreasonable that you spend your physical education time picking up acorns and pods.

Another good strategy is to not use academic time to discuss infractions of the rules that occurred on the yard at recess or lunch. It is very effective to discuss problems, in the classroom, during physical education time. Students waiting to get on the playground are eager to get a quick, effective solution to the problem and to make sure it doesn't happen again. Obviously if it happens again, even more time might have to be spent discussing rather than playing. Another simple but very effective solution is to seat two antagonists next to each other during physical education time. Tell them that you want them to have plenty of time to come to a reasonable solution.

There can be a chart in your room that lists cause and effect behavior situations. Because you should be most interested in students who are listening, paying attention, and staying on task, this chart deals with those issues. A cause could be disturbing the teacher or other students so that they could not concentrate on their work. The effect would be a checkmark per occurrence. Ten checks in one week result in a parent conference (on the phone first, or in person, if it seems more advisable). Ten checks or more a week for two consecutive weeks has the effect of the student not going to Reward Assembly. Reward Assembly at some schools occurs every other week for the fifth- and sixth-grade students. Or the effect can be an extra free playtime for forty-five minutes on Friday afternoons. Those not admitted to the playground go to a supervised classroom to study and work on material that will be helpful to them. Their teacher decides what area they need extra practice in or what makeup work might be necessary.

Every week, starting on Monday, there should be a fresh piece of paper on the teacher's desk. It is labeled "Behavior." There are no names on it. The first time a student causes a disturbance in the room, write down his or her name and one check. Each additional disturbance results in a check. This gives very accurate accounting for behavior grades on the report card and at parent conference time. Never comment at the time the check is placed on the sheet. This is advantageous in that it does not give the disturbers any extra attention by having their name called or everyone seeing it written on the board. This therefore becomes an efficient and considerate strategy. It helps the students see that the responsibility rests with them, no one else.

Many students grow in their self-respect when they have been able to change or modify their behavior to the point that they no longer have ten checks or more a week. For many it works like a charm. At the end of the day, some students will file by your desk to see how they are doing. Some quite restive students and some with learning disabilities seem to profit well from this strategy. About Wednesday or Thursday, you can see them trying to monitor their inattentiveness consciously. What more can a teacher ask? And it is so simple for the teacher. Your position is not one of an inefficient nag. You can also see rather quickly and objectively if there seems to be a pattern to inattentiveness: Are some days more difficult for an individual student than others?

VOICE EFFECTIVENESS

The voice is a powerful tool in classroom management. I have noticed that volunteers or very new student teachers are amazed that, after they have given directions to perform a task, no one has moved. Very specific directions need to be given in very clear, direct, sequential order. Occasionally, you need to say, "Do it now." Additionally, not over-talking is incredibly effective. By the time they reach what we refer to as upper grades (fifth and sixth), students must feel that they've suffered excessively from being talked to too much.

It is also a surprisingly effective control technique to simply put your hand out for the offending, disturbing toy. No long discussion then ensues as to that toy's special reason for being there at that place or at that time. Simply receive it in your hand and say immediately, "It will be on my desk for you to pick up after school today." Then smile and say thank you. Likewise for gum. No time is wasted or argument waged by saying, "Why are you chewing gum again? Don't you know it is against school rules? What are you thinking of?" Quietly say, "Please trash the gum," and nod your thanks and approval that it has been taken care of.

Students are very responsive to common courtesy when it is directed their way by the teacher. Try to remember to say please and thank you even when you are busy. The incredible power of *please* was brought home to a teacher several years ago when she was asked to take a student (an unknown student to her) from another classroom to the office. When she arrived in the requesting teacher's room, the errant student was standing at a table with his chair on the table in front of him. The teacher said he had to go to the office for punishment because he wouldn't put the chair down. So the newly arrived teacher said, "Put the chair down and sit down." He, being as tall as she was, stared her belligerently in the eye and didn't move. Suddenly, she realized she had been in too big of a hurry. She leaned toward him and very quietly said, "Please, put your chair down. I'd appreciate it if you'd please do that for me." Presto! The chair went down and he was sitting quietly!

It also saves a lot of time and a hoarse, strained voice if your class is used to having you give them hand signals for simple routine tasks. In the morning when you meet your class on the yard, you can wave a "come on in" with your hand. When there are up to ten classes in the auditorium, and it is time to leave, it is wonderful to have your class already trained. You don't have to try and get their attention. They are watching for your hand signal, and you are all off quickly and quietly.

The volume and intensity of the voice is also an incredibly powerful tool. By using your voice as a technique, you can produce a high level of attention and/or anticipation with loudness or softness. Since a good teacher probably only actually yells, or at least does what he or she considers yelling, at a class once a year, it is a very strong attention-getter.

The following ploy is also very effective. Use it when you become excessively perturbed about something. Either slam a book on the desk or the floor, or slam a door shut. Instantly, you have everyone's undivided attention without saying a word. Then, carefully keeping everyone in "eyeball range," speak in a whisper to explain the problem. It is important at this juncture to make sure that the needed change in the students does occur. Don't relax until it does. At that point, say, "Now that is the kind of class I thought was my room. I'm going to watch the clock to see if you can stay this fantastic for the next ten minutes." Then monitor them and the clock and again praise them.

SELF-ESTEEM

Self-esteem is now the catchall word in education, in magazine and newspaper articles, as well as in flyers promoting parenting classes. There are many who question what is being presented under the auspices of the idea of self-esteem. Is it possible that self-esteem has been overemphasized and responsibility ignored? The parenting and family influences, or lack thereof, have already taken place when the students arrive in the classroom. We cannot change that, but we can help make a difference. The values and techniques previously described do help.

SELF-ESTEEM THROUGH RESPECT
AND COURAGE

Self-esteem comes from being treated with respect. Teach your students that you will respect their opinions, even if they need to argue a point with you. Sometimes they win. Teaching them that they have the right to present a dissenting view and how to present it is a great technique for them to have and use.

An example: a new boy in the class politely points out to the teacher that he had incorrectly assumed another student was purposely being disruptive. (It became obvious that the teacher had erred.) The new boy is commended on his courage and the politeness and appropriateness of his approach. You can almost sense his feeling of worth in this new class. He is important, and the teacher will listen to him. Courage is an important part of self-esteem. Put a lot of emphasis on being courageous enough to stand up for what you feel is right, even if none of your peers agree.

SELF-ESTEEM THROUGH COMMUNITY AND BEING VALUED

Self-esteem means valuing oneself. When students have a strong sense of community within their classroom and are valued, they can value others in the room. This then extends to a larger environment. When students realize a girl in another room has been ignored and forgotten by her parents on her birthday, they ask permission to have materials and time to make the girl a birthday card. Their own self-esteem is good enough that they can be thoughtful and considerate of others.

Dr. Arthur Levine, chairman of the Institute of Educational Management at Harvard, emphasized community at the 1991 National Educator Awards. He spoke about the need to be a part of the larger community, and the importance of being responsible to others and having empathy and tolerance.

SELF-ESTEEM THROUGH A CROSS-AGE TUTORING PROGRAM

Self-esteem also comes from being responsible. A cross-age tutoring program teaches parenting and increases self-respect and responsibility at the same time. In the fall, you can arrange to have a kindergarten or first-grade classroom be "special friends" with your upper-grade class. Every student in your room has a special friend in the lower-grade classroom. Once a week, for twenty minutes, they visit the classroom and help their special friend. Students that previously had reputations as incorrigibles show a new dimension of their personalities. The responsibility assigned to them by you was to be caring of their special friend.

Suddenly you observe former bullies on their knees, cupping a new seedling in their hands, saying, "Now be careful with the roots. They're delicate." They are on their knees because they are planting the garden with their special friend, and they are getting close to eye level. Part of the preparatory work for your class has been to explain how tall they will appear to small five- and six-year-olds.

The importance of this program can be seen later when former students tell how they still help their special friends if they see them in the neighborhood. One former bully, in particular, came back from junior high several years in a row to make sure the program was still being continued since he felt it had been so important to him and his self-esteem. It is not unusual to discover a young child and his or her mother at your classroom door asking if they could please deliver some freshly baked cookies to a special friend. Another student was able to work out some of the pain she felt from a home situation. Her parents were discussing their problems and possible divorce with her. She wanted and needed more attention and consideration at that time. In giving her undivided attention to her special friend, she was able to forget her own troubles for awhile. She also reveled in the adoration her small special friend gave to her.

Listening attentively and with concentration is one of the tasks you need to ask your class to perform for their friends. Explain that it is a difficult task, for true listening, no matter how brief, requires tremendous effort. First of all, it requires total concentration. You cannot truly listen to anyone and do anything else at the same time. This is stated over and over in Dr. Scott Peck's books, and I heartily endorse the idea of good, focused listening skills as a special part of the education needed by young children. Listening attentively to their special friends gives them a chance to practice what you expect from them and, in turn, give to them. This is also relevant to one's self-concept. The point is often made that there is a connection between being listened to and feeling good about one's self. Students who are turned away from a speaker and who appear to be daydreaming while someone is speaking to them often are those that seem to be in need of a better sense of self.

25

CHOICES

There are times when the teacher realizes a power play is about to develop. Are you going to do what I ask you to do? You cannot always be sure you will win through pure power. It is the least effective tool and is inefficient in the amount of time it takes to play out the power scene. This is when a quick, off-the-cuff choice is needed. Part of the choice needs to be what you want the student to do and part has to be something that the student will envision as quite unacceptable.

An example: a student is talking more than you wish during a quiet lesson time. You have already indicated that the talking is disturbing by putting a check by his or her name and have quietly approached his or her seat and asked for more quiet. At that point ask the student to come into the hallway for a minute. Explain that the excessive talking is disturbing and since it has not stopped, he/she has several choices:

1. Be self-disciplined enough not to talk anymore to his/her tablemate for the next twenty minutes.
2. Find a place in the room to sit and work for twenty minutes where he/she won't be distracted.
3. Have you call home and ask that he/she finish the rest of the day at home or in another classroom.

The first option would not be given if there is no chance of it being an appropriate possibility. In other words, each situation has to be treated a little differently. A lot of knowledge about the student has to be immediately processed. You have to perform on-the-spot evaluations to be effective.

Another example involves a group of eight students. The noon-duty aide reports that the class was playing "rape" games at lunchtime. Knowing that the aide is rather strict and unforgiving, you do not immediately attend to the problem after lunch. Instead, just before the class goes home for the day, ask the eight offenders to write a letter explaining what had gone on. As you read the letters the next day at recess, your first free time, you see that they had indeed played a rough game with sexual overtones. One girl admitted that the zipper on her pants had been broken and that the boys were trying to take the girls' pants off.

Say nothing until just before lunchtime. Then announce that the eight involved students will wait in the classroom. After the other students have left for lunch, ask the eight to form a circle around a set of tables. At that time, reiterate what you have read from their papers that morning and speak of your concern about the possible severity of the problem. Conclude, "You have two choices: You may either go to lunch now and I will immediately be on the phone with your parents to discuss this with them, or you may give up a good half of your lunch time to hear me give you a lecture on sex, violence, and proper behavior." All opt to remain and listen. You then explain a few things about the differences between sexual acts, love, and violence and outline exactly the kind of behavior you expect from them during their lunch period.

There are no more reports of offensive games being played by the class. You may not hear from any parents, although you might. It seems that in our society, it is still a threat when a teacher says, "I will be calling your parent at work," that is, assuming that there is a parent who can be reached by phone.

26

STUDENTS WANT SPECIFIC GOALS

It does take time, planning, and willingness to say, "Yes, I am in charge. It is up to me to decide what direction to go and what values to insist upon." I discovered how important specific goals are to students the year I asked the adaptive physical education teacher for a copy of the physical fitness norms that are used nationally for the Presidential Physical Fitness Awards. Children have been competing for these awards since the seventies.

Every spring, all the fifth graders in Los Angeles have their scores on pull-ups, sit-ups, and the mile run recorded by their teachers. This data is then sent in to the district. The schools get a printout the following fall showing how well each student performed, and how well the school did in comparison with the larger population. If the boys and girls do not know exactly how many pull-ups are needed for success, they do not have the incentive to better themselves or to reach for a higher goal.

Since it is important for students to feel that their report card grades have validity, I would explain to them what the criteria were for an A, a B, or a C in P.E. on their report card. For one of their tri-semester grading periods, I would list on the board how many pull-ups and sit-ups were necessary, and the time in which a mile was to be run for a particular grade using the norms that I received from the adaptive physical education teacher. Additionally I had a bulletin board titled "How Phys-ically Fit Are You?" on the classroom wall all year. This was a working bulletin board that allowed me to chart the progress of the students from September, while they were practicing and increasing their strength and endurance, through springtime when they would be tested. During the year, I would add to the board photographs of those students who had attained the highest scores. Some students might shine in this area even though academic work was hard for them. It gave them a spot in the room that showed how they excelled. This bulletin board was a point of interest for the parents at the spring Open House, a time when they came to visit their child's classroom. It allowed them to see how their child was progressing according to national norms. I had explained the program to the parents in the fall, and I described how they could help their child develop physical fitness.

Since students like to be in charge of their grades and like specific goals, they performed better the year I started with these norms than they ever had before. It was amazing to see the increase in the scores from previous years. Other teachers with whom I worked liked the idea and involved their students. A year later, my school's scores were the highest they had ever been, beating out local schools and achieving higher ratings than the city in general.

(27)

THE NUTS AND BOLTS OF TEACHING

Thirty years of training student teachers for California State University, Northridge, taught me that there were certain very important principles that needed to be used in the classroom by student teachers if they wished to be successful. I have condensed my notes to my former student teachers into this "nuts and bolts" section. It is the basis for what makes it all work well.

There are three main components to teaching well, having students get the opportunity to strive toward their potential, and having a group of well-behaved, courteous students who are delighted to be at school. In a nutshell, these important elements are planning, timing, and consequences for behavior. Each part is equally important. They meld together to make the whole workable.

PLANNING

First, the teacher must prepare. This means planning what is to be taught and when, the organization of classroom procedures, and the development of effective lesson techniques. If a teacher is organized, the students have much less opportunity to get restless and to get into trouble.

Students are not as apt to be distracted when they are busy and realize that the assigned task is worthwhile.

That means that you, as the teacher, must be sure about the goal of your lesson. You must be aware of what you are trying to teach, how long it should take for the lesson to be completed, and what type of activity will best promote the learning you desire. It is not always possible to pinpoint to the minute how long it will take for a lesson to be finished. That is part of the art of teaching; therefore the good teacher will have fillers available. A filler, such as the spelling game Ghost, is a worthwhile use of an extra five minutes, and it keeps your class involved, which usually means well behaved.

Interruptions

The need for a worthwhile time-filler will also appear when there are classroom interruptions. Sometimes the office calls you or sends you a note, and other teachers and parents occasionally do the same. Plan with the class ahead of time what they are to do when that happens. It is always amazing how your students will want to start to talk the very minute you are required to give your attention to someone from outside of the classroom. It seems to be one of the laws of nature that has not yet been discovered, but it certainly is a truism.

Some of the specific tasks that you can plan for the children are to study spelling words, study vocabulary, or read a library book. This will not only help keep them quieter, but will lessen the opportunity for those who wish to poke their tablemate with a pencil or ruler, a favorite activity for boys and girls who don't have anything better to do and who feel they don't have anyone paying attention to them.

The Teacher's Job

It is important to be sure that you, as the teacher, know all components of the lesson. If you take too long trying to figure out a math problem on the chalkboard while the students have to wait, you will lose their attention. The same is true if the children have been asked to divide their spelling words into correct syllables. If you are looking up the words in the dictionary to check the syllables at the time they are working, it will be a waste of their time. This is work you should do as part of the lesson's preparation.

A great deal of balance is necessary when each day's work, the week's work, and the year's work are planned. For instance, when the year's curriculum in math is to be studied using an available textbook, you might decide that the only way to cover the material is to work on four pages a day.

It is important to remember that you need to have a philosophy of education for yourself that will allow you to know what you want to teach because the material and concepts are valuable. You will also need to know what to skip or delete because the work is irrelevant. Most teachers find that there is much more material that they want to cover in the school year than there are hours in that time period. In order for you to feel a sense of balance, and for the students to feel this same sense, you need to think about how to get all the concepts covered. Otherwise you will suspect that you did run away to the big top after all, and you are in charge of a three-ring circus.

As you plan the day be sure you include some excitement or drama in one of the lessons. There should also be a balance during the day of exciting new material and routine tasks. All lessons basically have a similar pattern. As the teacher, you will define the lesson's goal, give examples, let the students practice, and have time for correcting and evaluating. Although that is the basic lesson plan, each should have its own texture, taste, and seasoning. That is the creative part.

Clarity

It is incredibly important that all directions be given in a clear and concise manner. It is also valuable to give them in correct sequential order. Outlining the sequence of the task is an efficient way to get the student to work quickly. It seems to give children a sense of security to see the order in which they will attack a problem. A very good technique that makes the lesson's goal clearer is to have the boys and girls write it as a title at the top of their paper. For instance, *Decimals in Division* could be the title for a math paper.

If you decide to only give oral directions, be sure that they are clear and simple enough that you will not have to repeat them. More complicated directions may need to be written out on the board or charted ahead of time. This should not be done at length, while the student is just sitting, waiting, wondering what he or she needs to do.

When Should Directions Be Given?

Whether the assignment is for small groups, or for the group as a whole, always give the directions before the children need to move and go to other seats or the playground. Directions also need to be given before the students need to get out materials, such as texts, art supplies, or musical instruments. Be sure that the boys and girls know what to do before movement of any sort commences, otherwise many will not know what to do, and it will tend to be chaotic.

Evaluations

During the time that students are working, it is a good idea to walk around the room, to observe how they are progressing and make comments on their work to help them or encourage them. At the end of a lesson, be sure you know who does not understand the work and will need more help. It helps to make a little list showing the names of students who need more explanation or practice.

A super quick evaluation, though not perfect but good to use when your principal or supervisor appears, is to have the whole class quickly show if they understood a concept. The technique is to ask which of three or four answers is the correct one. If the correct answer is *a* the students put up one finger to indicate that. This is done with more fingers for *b* through *d*. Use it as a very quick evaluating device. It also has an advantage because everyone is directly involved at the same time. Pose the question, with the answers visible, and direct the boys and girls to have their hand in a fist as you say ready. Then as you say show, they put up the correct number of fingers. You can get some idea of who did not show an answer immediately, but waited to see what everyone else did. Obviously, if the whole class, or the majority, misunderstood, you are going to see that immediately.

Every year a teacher needs to evaluate the class's ability in order to assess the difficulty of material that is appropriate for that particular group. Ten years of teaching fifth graders can produce ten very different sets of boys and girls, each of which might need different material or different presentations of the curriculum.

Efficiency

A simple way to insure that students get to work rather than their taking time to discuss what went on before they got to school, or what happened on the recess or lunch break, is to put some work on the chalkboard before class begins in the morning and before you leave for your recess and lunch break. It takes time, but it is time well spent if you wish to have an orderly, relaxed classroom atmosphere.

I found that the morning started well if I had the children stand behind their chairs when they entered the room instead of sitting down. They would be participating in the flag salute before any other school business took place, and there was no reason to sit down and stand up again right away. When they sit down after the flag salute, the teacher needs a few minutes to take care of attendance, notes, and lunch count. That was when it was so helpful to have work already on the board for them. Make sure that if the work involves worksheets, you have placed those at their desks before they come in. All they have to do is put away their backpacks, sweaters, etc.; sit down; and go to work. That way, their time is not wasted while you take care of the clerical business for the morning.

Noisiness is distracting and can lead to more chaos. In some schools, students have to put the chairs on top of the desks at the end of the day so that the floor can be cleaned. It is best to have the chairs set down quietly. One can have the boys and girls practice picking up and setting down chairs quietly to show them that it is important that it is done that way.

Idiosyncrasies

We all have certain idiosyncrasies that we may not be aware of, but the students in the classroom quickly pick up on them. One year students were very upset with a substitute teacher who leaned over their desks to help them with their work. What he did not realize was that because he was so tall, and because the average classroom in Los Angeles is so crowded, his rear end was too close to the student seated at a desk behind him. The children thought this was funny and strange and gave the substitute less attentiveness due to this oversight on his part.

Although many idiosyncrasies are usually harmless, it is good to be cognizant or aware if you always end a sentence with the word *okay,* or stare at the ceiling, or stick out your tongue slightly while trying to figure out an answer to the question just posed by a student.

Test Integrity

There are procedures that you can develop to make things run more smoothly for the students while they are working. It is important to have test integrity in the room. Make it the testee's responsibility to make sure that his or her work is covered so that no one else, if they are looking around, can see the answers. Students can use books or a piece of paper to cover their test answers after they write them. This allows others to feel more comfortable about looking around the room while thinking about an answer.

This technique also does away with complaints from children that someone is cheating. During test time, walk around the room to remind students to cover their work. Only on a rare occasion will you need to add the consequence that if a testee does not keep their paper covered, points will be taken off their score.

Getting Attention

Getting the students' attention before they take out books or materials, or move to another area, has been emphasized. It seems to be the one most difficult principle for new teachers to apply. Get students' attention after they have finished a task by saying, "Please put your pencils down. Close your books. Look up here at the board now." Specific directions do get results. Then, be sure that their attention is kept on you and the lesson.

There is nervousness present when one first starts teaching, and I have noticed that student teachers will sometimes get the class working on a project and then remember something more that they wanted to say. If the student teacher, as often seems to happen, tells the students what else they are to do without getting the class's attention first, many children do not hear the instructions, and the boys and girls begin to feel that it is not important to listen to what is being said by the teacher.

Housekeeping

As students work, they amass material. Most elementary school desks are too small to hold work in progress, especially work that may take several weeks to finish. It is best to have the boys and girls make folders. The folders can be collected after a work period is over. This work can then be stored on a shelf in the classroom until it is ready to be used again. It also makes it easier for the teacher to take the folders to his or her desk, or home, to check on work in progress.

Distributing Materials

When you want folders or other materials passed out in class, you need systems to make it easy and routine. Students' time in class is precious, and it should not be wasted on mundane items. There are a number of ways to collect and pass out material. What works best for you, and is most efficient, is what you will use.

One method is to have a child in charge of passing out papers and materials. Another child might be in charge of collecting the work and materials. Sometimes, you can review the directions of north, south, east and west and have the students pass their work down a row to the west. Then it can be picked up and brought to the teacher by a designated boy or girl.

At the beginning, children may need help in passing papers down a row. There are a number of ways that they can make it take a lot of time and have it develop into a hassle. If you are unsure of the group's ability, have one row do it while everyone else watches. Explain exactly how you want it done and have that row show that it can be done that way. Then the other rows can do it as they have seen it demonstrated.

Discussions

It is important for students to feel that they are part of class discussions and will be called upon. Otherwise, some children will just daydream. Not all boys and girls want to participate. It seems to help the shy or uninterested when the teacher calls on students, one after the other, as they are sitting in a row. If they are warned that an answer is going to be expected, you can sometimes mark down whether the answer is exceptionally good, satisfactory, or poor. These lists then go into the grading system as extra credit and as information for their parents.

Using an expanded vocabulary with the students during discussions helps them become more aware of new words, their use, and meaning. *Horizontal* and *vertical* are good examples. If these terms are used when talking about turning a paper sideways, the students get an extra chance at increasing their vocabulary at the same time they are getting ready for a lesson. Every possible opportunity needs to be used to give them extra instruction.

Choices

Students seem to perform better and work harder if they are given a rationale as to why they should learn a subject or concept. Many children realize, at a fairly early age, what is a sensible use of their time. Showing the class that they have a choice in the direction they are going to take is a very effective tool. For example, you can sometimes say, "You may prepare a five-page outline of the chapter, and it will be graded, or you may read the material to understand it and write answers to the questions at the end of the chapter. You will be graded on how well you have answered the questions. Be careful to include all the information. You must, of course, put the answers into your own words. The second choice, which may only be a one- or two-page assignment, is a better use of your time."

The students then show by a hand count if they prefer to take the shorter task, which a good teacher feels will help them in the test they will be taking later in the week. They usually choose as one hopes they would and feel that they have some control over their day's learning activity. Lots of smiles on their faces sometimes show their satisfaction as they go to work.

TIMING

The second component is timing. Time is a very precious commodity in the classroom. It needs to be used efficiently and wisely. For instance, if students are always asking questions about directions that have just been given, you cannot teach, and they cannot learn. Senseless repetition can be a terrible waste of time. Some children just wish to have a lot of attention, and they will ask questions in which they have no interest in order to have everyone looking their way and listening to them. It is also a good idea not to repeat a child's oral answer after it has been given, as everyone should have heard it, and it just wastes time by repeating the same words over again.

Since not all boys and girls work at the same speed, plans can be devised so that faster students have enrichment work to participate in when they are finished, or a plan can be organized that will allow slower children to complete the work later.

The time one has in the classroom during the day needs to be balanced for the students as well as for the teacher. Students get tired, bored, and seem listless if they sit in one place too long, or do not have enough variety in their lessons.

Breaks

Children can be given a quick running break outside or time to get a drink of water, or a lesson can be arranged where everyone sits in their own seat for a work period, then changes to a cooperative group lesson where they have to get up and go to different chairs and tables.

At the end of the year, most school systems give standardized tests to the students. These tests involve a high level of focus from the child. After one section of the test is finished (in fifth grade that might be a forty-five-minute period), it is a good idea to give the boys and girls time to go to the bathroom, get a drink, and take a short run to release their tension. Running is a good tension reliever, and students appreciate being able to relieve the stress they might feel. It is a good technique that they can continue to use in their lives. Another technique is to have the students bring their papers to you when the work period is over. You can often call for their papers by name, alphabetically, and this gives them a few moments' respite from work, and a little bit of physical movement.

Teachers also need to pace themselves during the day. It works well to have an intense directed lesson with a lot of new material being presented by the teacher followed by a period where the students will be working quietly on their own at their desks. This gives the teacher a chance to catch his or her breath, and to regroup mentally for the next assignment.

Voice

If a teacher is hurried or harassed, the students hear it in his or her voice and get noisy themselves. Quite often, I have been surprised when student teachers who had good voice control when I observed their lessons would lose that strong voice quality when their college supervisor came in. Their voice would then quaver and lose resonance. The students noticed this right away, and they became less attentive. It was easy for me to reassure the student teachers that there was no reason for concern if I had faith in them, and gradually they would become more confident and regain a good voice to use with the class when they had a visitation from their college professor.

Time to Clean Up

Art projects involve a lot of material and a lot of cleanup time. Art is probably the most difficult of all subjects to close without having chaos develop. I found that my energy was best in the morning and developed that as my art period.

It helps to have a crew who is responsible for certain parts of the cleanup. Washing paintbrushes and tidying up paper and crayons are tasks better done by a few than by everyone. Every person needs to clean up their own place to make it ready for the next assignment, and the special art crew then has room and time to get the materials in order for a new project.

Students want to finish whatever they are working on, but they don't always have an awareness of how much time is left to complete a task. It seems like common courtesy to warn the children that their time will be over in ten to fifteen minutes. It is good to put the time when a project needs to be finished on the chalkboard for the class. Remind them that they only have a little time left, for if they are working hard, they are not watching the clock. That is the teacher's job.

Attention-getters

I suspect that when one subject period is finished, the students automatically release tension by talking. It is amazing how often a teacher will say, "Close your books," and immediately as the books are being shut the conversation begins. This can be a release for a few minutes if the class will quickly give the attention back to the teacher.

Several attention devices can be used in the classroom to get the boys and girls to turn toward the teacher and to listen. Sometimes a class is quiet enough or responsive enough that one just has to ask them for their attention. At other times, there may be two classes in a room for a special project, and flicking the lights on and off is a better signal if a voice may not be heard. The light signal has to be explained to the students and practiced before it is effective. In primary grades, especially kindergarten, a small bell is often rung to get the children's attention when they are in work areas. They then stop working, look at the teacher, and wait for directions.

On the playground, it is satisfying if your class, which may be spread out over several diamonds or play areas, can come when you blow your whistle. One can use different signals with a whistle. One short blast will notify them that the physical fitness area at which they have been practicing needs to be left, and the next one has to be tried. A special "toot-to-to-toot-toot" blow of the whistle means that their sports time is up, and it is time to line up for drinks and a return to the classroom.

CONSEQUENCES OF BEHAVIOR

The last component is a well-behaved classroom. Good planning and thoughtful timing often result in a class's good behavior. When a teacher knows all the elements of a lesson and is well prepared, he or she can give the boys and girls the eyeball contact that is needed to keep them on task.

When students do not work well, are too noisy, or are disruptive during some part of the lesson, one good technique is to wait until the next day, or the next lesson, to explain that you are aware of the problem. Tell the children in detail what is expected and emphasize that it is important that the correct procedure be followed. Then the class has a chance to practice under your watchful eye. Then when it is good to slow down the pace and make sure that what you have asked them to do is being done correctly. If they need more practice, that is the time for the practice is right then. Occasionally you will say to a class, "Where is that great class that I was so proud of? I know they were here yesterday." At the same time have your hand above your eyebrows and scan the room. This helps break the tension for the teacher as well as the class.

It is good to remember that many of the students may be doing just what they are supposed to do. If they feel they are being reprimanded when they have not done anything wrong, they feel a sense of unjustness, and rightly so. If the teacher yells or castigates the whole class for what a few did, the teacher ends up with many children feeling upset. To separate the infraction and the person or persons involved from those who are doing what they are supposed to do, it is best to talk with the boy or girl, or the group of students, entangled in the problem out of earshot of the others.

Do not get caught up in a personal challenge from an obstreperous child with an ensuing power play while the class is carefully monitoring the verbal jousting. It is not good for the teacher, or the student or students involved in misbehaving, and it is certainly not good for the class.

The children are then torn between wanting to be on the teacher's side and their classmate or friend's side. It is not fair to put boys and girls into that position.

Consequences

Consequences do occur in life. Cause and effect is even listed as one of the concepts students are to be aware of when they are reading. Consequences should be legitimate educational study tasks. I do not believe that writing "I will not chew gum," or whatever school rule was broken, is as effective as having students copy a page or more out of one of their textbooks in cursive writing. Many boys and girls need practice in cursive writing, and it often seems that the student who ends up with the need for discipline consequences has almost un-readable handwriting. Another worthwhile activity is to have them outline the paragraphs on a page or two of one of their textbooks. Some teachers will use recess time or the playtime after lunch for this activity. P.E. time should not be used, as students must have physical education instruction or participation for twenty minutes a day in California. It is one of the few subjects that have a definite time man-dated by the state.

You can develop a special play-day period as a reward for those who have finished classwork and homework at an acceptable level. Keep a record of who has not been satisfactory in their work habits and who has not answered questions in class when that was the task. When the chil-dren have been assigned material to read, have been given time to take notes, and have time to answer questions in writing in order to be pre-pared to give verbal answers, one can keep a checklist of those who are not prepared. At the end of two weeks, you can make a list of boys and girls who will be rewarded with extra time after their physical education period.

This responsible group will get to choose from an assortment of games that are only available at this reward time. They can play with a Hacky Sack, badminton birds from Australia, a miniature golf set, Fris-bees, Ping-Pong paddles at the handball court, or just have extra time to play chess for fun. The consequence for the students who do not earn the reward is to sit at an outside lunch table with special assigned work that is directly developed for their individual needs. Each boy or girl sits at a different table, as this is not a time for them to socialize or to be interested in anyone else's work. This takes extra teacher time, but the children do realize that you think enough of them to give individualized relevant work, even though the consequences have not been a reward. This works as a motivational tool for many students, but not all.

Old Habits

Sometimes a teacher needs to respond immediately to an undesired response from the children. If students had previously, in last year's grade, gotten into the habit of moaning when the teacher asked for the math or social studies books to be opened, it is a habit that needs to be nipped in the bud right away. Smile the first time that happens in a class and explain that they can think whatever they wish. You will not monitor that, but they are not to voice their feelings out loud. The next time that book needs to be opened, remind them, ahead of time, of the guidelines that have been set up. When an old habit has to be changed, it does take some reminding and practice to develop new patterns.

Questions

I do not think that it is a good idea to ask students the question "Did you like that lesson?" Some student teachers will do this, and it opens up the opportunity for the class mischief maker to get the floor and make a lot of irrelevant noise and comments. The teacher or student teacher doesn't have much validity in stopping the boy or girl, as they asked for it.

It is the student teacher's job to ask insightful questions that lead to exploration and development of ideas. The urge to be liked and to get reassurance from students is what seems to lead new teachers in the training stage to ask the class as a whole for personal encouragement. If a teacher is sure about the validity of the lesson being taught and has tried to present it in a creative, interesting way, he or she should feel satisfied that the job is being done correctly.

Permission for Students to Leave the Classroom

Fewer classroom problems will arise if a teacher does not send two students who tend to get into trouble together on an errand or excuse them to go to the bathroom at the same time. Each school has its own rules concerning bathroom visits during class time. Some schools insist that students wait until recess, lunch, or dismissal time, unless it is an emergency. Emergencies are not always easy to ascertain. Knowing the students and how reliable they are is the best way to determine if an emergency is real. A teacher has to use intuition and common sense.

Know that giving a class a break from the routine of sitting still during a long study period of several hours can be beneficial in several ways. Give them a "fresh-air break" of about ten minutes. The class goes outside, and they have the choice of running, getting a drink, or going to the bathroom. It is also a good time to answer any questions that have come up while they were working but had not gotten around to asking.

Since most schools frown on students being excused to go to the bathroom from the classroom, this is a good solution. Because the children are under your supervision, the problem of possible vandalism in the bathroom is taken care of, the time is monitored, and everyone seems ready to work more efficiently when they return to the classroom.

Squabbles

Sometimes, two or more boys or girls will have had a quarrel or misunderstanding on the yard at recess or lunchtime. They usually want to assign blame and tell their story at great length. It saves a lot of time, and reduces the number of students who wish to get attention by always complaining unnecessarily about others, if you ask the children who are involved to write down everything that happened.

Give the quibblers paper from the recycling bin and have them sit away from each other or anyone else while they are writing. If you seat them near their classmates, it might cause a disturbance as it is natural to show someone what you have written, and the classmate might be interested in looking at the complaint. Collect the complaints, read them, act upon them, and tell the students that you will keep what they have written as evidence if anyone needs to know about the incident.

This means that the written complaint is available to the principal or parents. If the writing is not up to grade-level standards, ask the boy or girl to go back and edit it for correctness until it is acceptable. This is very effective. Children are more selective when they complain about minor infractions after they have the experience of correctly writing up what has happened. I suspect when they see their complaint in writing, it might not seem to be such a big deal.

Unresolved Irritations

Some children will come into a new classroom in the fall filled with the former semester's unresolved irritation at another student. Imagine a girl who had been in the habit of always complaining about a boy. Her hand was constantly up in order to tell about a problem concerning him. It appeared that she wanted to get him into trouble. When you check with the previous year's teacher, you find that this had been a habit pattern in that grade.

You can reverse the effect. When the girl complains, get after her for not doing her work and for disturbing the class. Instead of reprimanding the boy and moving him, move the girl. A good teacher will have been watching the two children carefully in order to be sure that she was indeed complaining unnecessarily. One might suspect that she has a home situation where she does not feel that there is fair treatment for herself, and she wants to prove that she can win. Changing the girl's behavior pattern is very effective. She can become more focused on her work, as complaining does not have positive feedback for her.

Calm Days

Many teachers have observed that their class is calmer on some days of the week than other days. You might see that the students are quietest, as a rule, on Mondays. By Wednesday, they seem to be more restless and more inclined to talk. Knowing this, plan the dates for play productions or field trips on their quieter days. Again, it is surprising how much classroom behavior can stem from teacher thoughtfulness and planning.

Courtesy and Civility

Courtesy and protecting students from feeling left out also leads to better classroom behavior. It is unwise for the teacher to forget to plan well. An example is when there is a need to divide the class into smaller groups. Thoughtful planning will mean that the teacher has arranged the groups so that no child feels caught in the "last one to be chosen syndrome." If that syndrome is operating in a classroom, the child so designated may want to act out his or her hurt and frustration, the other students will tend to comment, and those who are not yet careful of others' feelings will start to tease. None of this leads to a secure, cooperative group. All it takes is planning and consideration to keep this from happening. Sometimes you can use the classroom seating arrangement for groupings. Explain that all of the students in Row 1 and Row 3 will make up one group, with Rows 2 and 4 making up the second group. Another day change the groupings so that Rows 1 and 2 work together and Rows 3 and 4 work together.

This is the same kind of courtesy and thoughtfulness that needs to be expressed by the teacher for the students when an answer or directions need to be given to only one boy or girl. The teacher should speak quietly or in a whisper so that others are not disturbed while working. Educators need to be an example of the consideration they expect from the students in the class.

Children's feelings also need to be protected when student-developed material is to be read out loud to the class. It is best for the teacher to read it or to ask the child who wrote it to read. When another boy or girl is asked if they want to read someone else's work, they might refuse. That would cause embarrassment for a member of the class, which is not necessary or fair.

Classroom Control

Good classroom control makes for a class that the teacher wants to be with. It results in a classroom where the students feel they are treated with fairness, concern, and efficiency. This does not happen immediately. During one's first few weeks at the new school, students need to be sure that their teacher means what he or she says, and that he or she is going to pay attention to see if they are following directions. It usually takes up to three weeks, on average, for most groups to get to the stage where they understand the rules, accept the rules, and generally feel good about how their classroom is run.

It is much easier and quicker to achieve this ideal when the instructor has been at the school for a number of years. I did have respect and attention from the students and community at the school where I had taught for twenty-two years. When I moved to a new school for my last ten years, I found that, although I knew what to do and how to do it, it was a process that took much longer. It took almost a year at my new school before the boys and girls stopped asking me if I would be back the next year.

Effectiveness Is Reinforcement

It seems sad, but true, that good classroom discipline has to be reinforced and cannot be ignored. I suspect the lesson here is that you have to keep up your energy and attention. Maintaining discipline is a demanding job, but a supremely fulfilling job. In many instances the students' behavior reflects how you, as their teacher, have integrated the techniques discussed in planning goals and timing. They are incredibly interrelated. Much good behavior is simply what happens when you are on top of the daily goals and timing for the class.

THE MANY COMPONENTS OF TEACHING

A teacher can have control of a class temporarily, and have educational objectives for the day, but still not teach anything unless planning has taken place. Planning is needed on how to teach the objectives and what materials might be needed. Even a simple task, such as preparing for the class to tear a piece of paper into four or eight sections for a game, can involve a lot of directions and a need for awareness on the instructor's part as to what the difficulties or hang-ups might be.

Picture a new educator telling the class that they are going to need small pieces of paper for a math or vocabulary game. The paper that will be torn into smaller pieces has to be passed out and the directions given. Experience allows a teacher to know that the students may hold the paper the wrong way before folding it, and that might make a difference if everyone's paper pieces have to be the same size. Then, experience will remind one that some children may lick their papers after they fold them in order to tear them more easily. It is not a good idea for classmates to be using paper that someone else has licked, so that has to be addressed. Some boys and girls might become very frustrated at uneven edges or mistakes. Unless there is a need for perfection, you do not want to keep passing out paper, as that can be a game in itself for the students. They will also want to know what to do next at each step, and will become frustrated if they are not sure what they are to do.

Since there is only one teacher, or one teacher and an aide, in most classrooms, it is sometimes a good idea to allow quick achievers to help others. Those finished with the task may leave their seats and go where help is needed. They love to have that opportunity. Those sitting at the same desk or close by can also help each other.

It is the instructor's job to question and to be reflective. An educator has to ask what he or she wants to teach, what is wanted from and for each student, how to use time efficiently, and how to get energy and zest into some lessons. Then it all comes together.

EPILOGUE

These strategies work. Abraham Mazlow, a prominent educational psychologist, pointed out that we do not climb out onto the next higher branch until we are secure where we are. Time and time again, on field trips, the students in my classes have been complimented on their kindness to each other. One year that meant being able to share generously some very exciting binoculars, microscopes, and marine specimens at the Malibu Lagoon. It all works.

Students, parents, and teachers all need a high level of success and security in schools. The tried and tested techniques presented in this book should be available to all. Students should be able to reach their individual potential in a secure and challenging environment. Their parents should want the best for them and try to promote that which will benefit their children. Teachers should be eager to approach each new day with their classroom of equally eager students. It is my hope that this book will help others to attain the bliss in their careers that Joseph Campbell, the famed writer and educator, has led us to strive for.

REFERENCES

Fischer, D. H. (1989). *Albion's Seed*. New York: Oxford University Press.

Ignas, E., and R. J. Corsini (1981). *Comparative Educational Systems*. Chicago: University of Chicago Press.

Morris, Campbell (1988). *More Best Paper Aircraft*. New York: Perigee.

Peck, S. (1978). *A Road Less Traveled*. New York: Simon and Schuster.

Rohlen, T. P. (Winter 1985/1986). "Japanese Education: If They Can Do It, Should We?" *The American Scholar* vol. 55, no. 1.

Schultz, S. K. (1973). *The Culture Factory: Boston Public Schools, 1789–1860*. New York: Oxford University Press.

Stone, N. (March/April 1991). "Does Business Have Any Business in Education?" *Harvard Business Review*.

U.S. National Commission on Excellence in Education. *A Nation at Risk: The Imperative for Educational Reform*. Washington, DC: GPO, 1983.

White, M. (1987). *The Japanese Educational Challenge: A Commitment to Children*. New York: Free Press.

Wilson, D. (Winter/Spring 1986). "What Is the Teacher's Television Image?" *Delta Kappa Gamma Bulletin* vol. 52.

ABOUT THE AUTHOR

Darlene Anderson Wilson, whose career spanned the last half of the twentieth century, has spent thirty-eight years as a teacher, acting principal, and training teacher in elementary schools in the Los Angeles Unified School District. Her experience shows how a classroom teacher can promote an atmosphere where the students not only succeed academically, but are eager to do their best while concentrating on the basic values of responsibility, respect, consideration, and sensitivity.